*in your dreams
essentials

edwin raphael

foulsham
LONDON • NEW YORK • TORONTO • SYDNEY

foulsham
The Publishing House, Bennetts Close, Cippenham,
Slough, Berkshire SL1 5AP, England

ISBN 0–572–02759-1

Copyright © 2002 W. Foulsham & Co. Ltd

Cover illustration by Jurgen Ziewe

All rights reserved.

The Copyright Act prohibits (subject to certain very
limited exceptions) the making of copies of any copyright work
or of a substantial part of such a work, including the making of
copies by photocopying or similar process. Written permission
to make a copy or copies must therefore normally be obtained from
the publisher in advance. It is advisable also to consult the
publisher if in any doubt as to the legality of any copying
which is to be undertaken.

Printed in Great Britain by The Bath Press, Bath

Introduction

From the earliest recorded history – and surely even before then – to the 21st century, people have been fascinated by dreams. What influences the subject of our dreams? How can they sometimes appear to be so real while at the same time offering images that can be so startling or even weird? Are they trying to tell us something? And if so, what? Could they be messages from God or from a higher power? Or are they just a random combination of images from our daily lives restructured by our subconscious into surreal juxtapositions?

From the treatises of ancient theologians to the works of modern psychologists, much has been written on the subject of our dreams. The aim of this book is to provide a straightforward and modern explanation of the traditional interpretation of classic dream images, so that you have access to a clearly presented reference to the meanings of your dreams. Once you have established that meaning, you can give serious consideration to whether or not it can be useful to you in your waking life. Perhaps your subconscious mind actually has a simple solution to a problem that is baffling your conscious mind. Perhaps your dreams can highlight areas of your life that need attention, things you have been trying to avoid or feelings you have been working to suppress. It is possible that they can offer some insight into your circumstances or motivation. They may even point you in directions that will improve the quality of your waking life. The crucial point is that it is up to you to make things happen in your life – whatever your dreams may suggest. Doing nothing is just as much of a choice as taking action, but it will inevitably mean that you don't achieve exactly what you want.

Of course, what you dream about, and how you interpret those dreams must – to a certain extent – be subjective. If a mother of a young child dreams of that child starting school, it may simply be because that event is preying on her mind. Thinking about what happens in the dream and how she will cope with the event when it does come can help her to deal effectively and sensitively with what is a major event in the lives of both her and her child. If an elderly woman were to dream the same dream, however, it may suggest that she needs to review the events of her life, or perhaps feels a greater need for contact with the young, or yearns for a new direction.

Most dreams will combine a range of images, but it is those that are most prominent that should draw your attention and give you pause for thought. If you cannot find an appropriate interpretation in the first place you look, try looking up other words for the same image, or related images, and you should find a reference to give you guidance. For example, if you dream about an oak tree, you might look under Oak tree, Tree, Forest or Leaf. It is also worth considering the juxtaposition of images – a common occurrence in dreams – which can sometimes suggest deeper or more complex meanings.

Remember also that if the dream has a negative connotation, this does not mean that what is suggested will actually happen. Dreams reflect what is happening to you at the time, so if a dream indicates a potentially low time for you, you have it in your power to alter that by making a change in your actions,

Introduction

your attitude or your circumstances. It may only require a small shift in direction to nudge your fortunes back on to a more positive course.

Because we are all unique, only you can place your dream images in context and find the meaning that is special to you, a meaning you can apply to your life to make an improvement in some way. These interpretations may give you some guidance in that task. Sleep well.

Abscess

An abscess or boil is a significant image of a problem or troublesome issue that is concerning you. If you have it lanced, the dream therefore suggests that you could have the solution to the problems in your hand.

Absent friend

If you dream of feeling sadness over someone's absence, it is generally thought to be an indication that the person will soon come back into your life and that your relationship may well be significantly strengthened. If you are feeling happy that they are out of your life, you may receive unexpected and not particularly welcome news.

Abundance

To dream that you have an overabundance of anything is generally considered a bad image in a dream. This suggests that you are taking things too much for granted and you may find that you soon begin to lack that of which you appear to have so much.

Abyss

An abyss, crevice or cavern figuring significantly in a dream is generally thought to suggest that you may be looking into the unknown, but it does not necessarily mean that things will turn out badly.

Acacia tree

This is a traditional symbol of good news, suggesting expanding and blossoming horizons. *See also* Tree.

Accident

An accident in a dream is generally thought to be indicative of a major event likely to happen in your life, which could be either pleasant or unpleasant. Perhaps you are anxious about something you are undertaking and need to review the arrangements in order to feel more secure that it will work out well.

Accounts

Care should be exercised if you dream of accounts or account books, as there is a suggestion that something in your financial dealings needs attention, something that is preying on your mind. You may already be aware of some discrepancy that needs to be addressed.

Acorn

Acorns are omens of money and happiness. The potential is there to be realised. *See also* Oak tree.

Acrobat

The symbol of an acrobat suggests balance and physical control. Be wary that you do not lose yours and have an accident.

Acting

To dream that you are acting suggests that you may have to push yourself forward more than usual in order to obtain what you want.

Actor

Dreaming of an actor signifies that you may have doubts about the sincerity of someone close to you.

Admirer

To dream that someone is admiring your looks is an indication that a particularly dear wish is likely to be fulfilled. To dream that you are admiring someone else but that they are not aware of it can indicate that others may be able to deceive you as to their intentions.

Adoption

If you have a dream in which you have been adopted, it is a suggestion that you may soon be parted from a parent or from someone close to you. If you dream of adopting a child, this suggests that you are likely to be taking on new responsibilities before very long.

Adultery

A dream in which you commit adultery suggests an unclear conscience or a tendency to be argumentative, although if you are tempted and resist, this underlines your strength of purpose, which does not necessarily have to be related to any sexual matters.

Advertisement

Reading the advertisements in a newspaper or magazine suggests that you are about to draw attention to yourself, perhaps through the written word. Answering an advertisement in a dream suggests that you are looking for something to alter in your life and could soon experience a change in your circumstances.

Advice

To receive advice, either good or bad, from a supposed friend could indicate that someone is working against you, probably while pretending to be on your side, although this may not necessarily be the person you see in the dream.

Affectation

Seeing people behaving in an affected manner suggests things may be contrary to how they appear. Look more closely at circumstances surrounding you and try to get the facts straight before you make important decisions.

Agate

Agates or semi-precious stones are symbolic of a sense of sadness.

Age

To dream that you have grown to a ripe old age suggests honesty and contentment. If you see yourself having a relationship with a much older person, it is generally suggestive of financial success.

Agreement

If you are involved in business and dream about entering into an agreement, your business could suffer from a general downturn in trade or as a result of other people's failure. Be particularly careful in the arrangements you make at work.

Airship

To see yourself in a stationary airship suggests that you will have little success in life unless you work hard to get out of the rut into which you have fallen. If the airship is moving very quickly, be wary of investing your money, as this dream suggests potential losses, since the natural movement of an airship is slowly and under control.

Algebra

To be working at algebra in a dream signifies that any speculations you are involved in are likely to be successful as you are applying the right techniques of an analytical mind to achieve your ends.

Almond

Seeing or eating almonds can be an indication that you will have to face difficulty or disappointment in the not-too-distant future, especially if the almonds taste bitter. The traditional interpretation of seeing almond trees in a dream is that your hard work – symbolised by the hard nuts – will be rewarded. *See also* Nut, Tree.

Alone

Being alone in a dream is usually considered to be a dream of contrary, suggesting that you have influential friends.

Altar

To find yourself at an altar is an image of joy, although if you turn your back on the altar, it can suggest that you should review your attitude or your intentions, in case they lead you away from happiness and success.

Ancestor

A dream in which you see your ancestors is traditionally thought to suggest possible accidents, if you are not more careful. However, perhaps someone may be watching over you.

Anchor

An anchor is a symbol of a firm foundation, trust and hope.

Angel

Seeing an angel in a dream is a positive and life-enhancing image, suggesting a long and happy life with support from those close to you. It is obviously not good, however, if you argue with or reject an angel. This could indicate that you are aware that you are rejecting the advice or support of someone who cares for you or could be helpful to you.

Anger

Anger in a dream symbolises enemies and conflict, although not necessarily with the person appearing in your dream. Take care to avoid arguments, and make sure that no one is trying to undermine you by making unfair comments behind your back.

Angling

Think about whether there is something you really want and how hard you are prepared to work to obtain it. If you are battling with a fish on the end of a line, and especially if you are pulled in, you may encounter some stiff opposition to your plans, or find that someone is working against you. *See also* Fish, Fisherman.

Animal

Peaceful grazing animals are suggestive of successful business dealings. However, if you are attacked by wild animals in a dream, you may encounter hypocrisy among supposed friends or colleagues. If you dream that you have the head of an animal, you are envisaging that you have the strength and qualities of that animal and can use them to good effect. *See also* individual animals.

Ant

Ants are usually symbolic of hard work and industry, and watching a swarm of ants working in a dream suggests that you are likely to benefit from hard work yourself. However, if they are swarming over your body, this is a negative image as it suggests stress or even ill health.

Ape

Dreaming of an ape is said to indicate that you are aware of deceit in someone close to you. *See also* Animal.

Applause

Receiving applause is not necessarily a positive dream image. It can simply mean that you will either cause or be involved in some disruption, although this can be either positive or negative, depending on the circumstances.

Apple

Seeing or eating tasty apples suggests pleasure, enjoyment and success, although a sour apple indicates the opposite: arguments and disagreements. If you are picking apples in your dream but not eating them, it can suggest that you are looking for pleasure but being blocked in some way, and perhaps you are annoyed that someone is preventing you from getting what you want. If you dream that you are giving apples to someone else, it is a positive symbol of sharing and trust.

Trees are a positive dream image, and seeing an apple tree, especially if it is coming into bloom, and if you are feeling low, is an encouraging sign that things are likely to improve. *See also* Fruit, Tree.

Apricot

To see or eat fresh apricots denotes good health and pleasure. Fruit trees are almost always a positive dream image, and an apricot tree suggests pleasure and contentment, especially if it is healthy and loaded with fruit. If it is blossoming or bearing fruit out of season, you may experience an unexpected success. On the other hand, if the fruit is rotten or diseased, it may suggest that you are giving in too much to laziness and need to exert more energy to achieve what you want. *See also* Fruit, Tree.

Argument

An argument in a dream, especially if it is a violent argument and you hear people swearing and abusing each other, suggests that you could experience some bad luck in the near future since you are clearly concerned about confrontation or disputes of some kind. Be as sensible and reasonable as you can after such a dream to avoid giving anyone the opportunity to take advantage of you. It could be that you need to listen more carefully to your business colleagues, or that it is time to be more thoughtful and attentive to your partner or family. *See also* Discussion, Quarrel.

Arm

A dream in which you are more than usually conscious of your arms can have a variety of interpretations. If your arms are bigger and stronger than normal, it suggests that you will have the support of your family and this may help you to become successful and happy, but if your arms are thin or broken, your present course of action may lead to difficulties or unhappiness.

Army

To see an army of soldiers indicates a feeling that you find yourself in a set of circumstances over which you have no control.

Arrest

To dream of being arrested is an image suggesting that you anticipating impending difficulties. Try to take a fresh view of the circumstances surrounding you and see if you can find other ways of proceeding that will be more profitable.

Asleep

Especially if you are busy person, to dream that you are falling asleep or finding it hard to stay awake is not difficult to interpret as it is a hint that you need to take some rest. If you do not, it is possible that you may be working very hard but accomplishing little because you are not giving the job your full attention. *See also* Tiredness.

Astonishment

If the overall feeling in your dream is one of astonishment at any event, it is likely that you will experience some surprising changes in your life.

Asylum

To dream that you are in an asylum suggests that you may have to take on new responsibilities. You are likely to find unusual or unexpected ways to cope with those responsibilities or to avoid any difficulties you may be experiencing, and may even become famous through some great achievement.

Athlete

This image in a dream signifies that you have the energy required to face adventurous undertakings or business negotiations.

Atlas

To dream that you study an atlas is an image that suggests you are likely to increase your connections with foreign people or places.

Attack

A dream about being attacked shows conflict and concern. Try to resolve any outstanding arguments and make sure other people are not trying to undermine your position.

Auction

Make sure you can trust all those who call themselves your friends after dreaming of a situation in which everything simply goes to the highest bidder.

Autumn

If a dream is set in the autumn, it suggests established happiness at home. The atmosphere is likely to suggest calm and a restful time.

Avarice

To dream that you are avaricious or if you witness other people's greed indicates that you could be in danger of losing your money by foolish speculation if you continue on your present course.

Avenue

A dream involving a long, wide, perhaps tree-lined avenue suggests that you are seeking an understanding with someone who is very important to you and that you can see your way forward to achieving that understanding.

Baby

A baby can be seen as an image of new life or of responsibility. If the baby is healthy and happy, look for new opportunities to exploit to your advantage. If the baby is ill, however, you could anticipate a turn of events that increases your responsibilities.

Back

To dream that someone's back is injured or even broken signifies mockery and subjection.

Backgammon

Playing backgammon in a dream suggests that you have it in mind to become more studious, perhaps take up an educational course or master a new skill. *See also* Chess, Draughts, Game.

Bag

Carrying a full bag in a dream suggests that you are always likely to have what you need, although perhaps not as much as you might want. Carrying an empty bag suggests approaching difficulty with finances, or that you may have to do without something you want. If the bag is so full that it is impossible to close it, you might even find that you have so much money or so many possessions that you find it difficult to protect them or to use them wisely.

Bagpipes

Wind instruments such as bagpipes tend to indicate contention, perhaps with legal connotations. *See also* Music.

Bailiff

Dreaming that the bailiffs come to seize your property for debt is a dream of contrary, suggesting a windfall or some unexpected but favourable change of circumstances. If the dream is repeated more than once, however, it has the opposite meaning. *See also* Debt.

Baker

This is a very positive dream image. You may expect whatever plans you have put into place to be successful. *See also* Baking, Bread, Cake.

Baking

Baking bread or cakes suggests homely comforts and even unexpected happiness. *See also* Baker, Bread, Cake.

Bald

If you dream that you are bald or growing bald, especially if you are a woman, it suggests that you feel a sense of impending loss. *See also* Hair, Shaving.

Ball

Enjoying yourself at a ball or dance relates to the circumstances of your love life. If you are dancing with the right partner, then this implies that your relationship will go well and you are likely to be happy together. However, if you dream that you are dancing with the most attractive person in the room, rather than your own partner, it suggests that you should be more cautious, as you could be in for a difficult time with one of your acquaintances. Perhaps someone may try to break up your relationship, so be wary.

Balloon

To dream of an ascent in a balloon suggests that you may have to stoop pretty low to gain what you want, but luck should be on your side and you are likely to be successful.

Banana

A good omen, eating a banana in a dream indicates happiness and success should be yours for the taking. *See also* Fruit.

Bank

Visiting a bank in a dream underlines concerns of a financial nature, which could be to do with your personal finances or with business. It is a suggestion that you should be cautious in your dealings with money.

Banns

To dream that you are listening to your own banns of marriage being read out in church is indicative of good times and popularity ahead.

Banquet

A dream of a banquet suggests prosperity, although if you attend but do not eat anything, then you may be missing out on advantages from which others benefit.

Baptism

To be present at a baptism is an omen of riches or success in love, as it signifies new beginnings and belonging to a protective and influential group. *See also* Font.

Barefoot

To go on a journey barefoot is a sign of prosperity, possible travel and meeting influential people.

Barn

To see a barn filled with corn suggests success, but if the barn is empty and deserted, you could experience problems, especially financial ones.

Barrel

A barrel of beer in your dream generally indicates carelessness. Have you become careless of your health, overindulgent, or have you ignored advice to improve your diet or lifestyle? Have you started taking medication that you really know is not going to do you any good? Look to your general habits and see if they can be improved.

Bat

A bat flying about in the dusk suggests that you could find yourself in a situation in which you distrust the motives or veracity of someone with whom you come into contact. It can also suggest spiritual uncertainty or an instinctive fear that you need to come to terms with. *See also* Animal.

Bath

Dreaming of a bath of water that is too hot to get into is symbolic of having to overcome difficulties. However, washing in clear water suggests doing away with past difficulties and overcoming problems. *See also* Washing.

Bay tree

The bay is considered a bitter herb, and is therefore traditionally associated with failure, although this can be influenced by how you relate to the herb in your waking life. It may be that the experience of a minor failure or difficulty is what you need to spur you on to success, or to redirect your energies towards a more profitable or valuable venture. *See also* Herb.

Bear

A bear in a dream is generally thought to indicate a powerful and perhaps cruel enemy. *See also* Animal.

Beard

Dreaming that your beard has been pulled or cut off suggests that you should be on the alert for some difficult circumstances in the near future. On the other hand, if you seem to have a rich and luxuriant beard, it suggests financial success.

Bee

Bees are a symbol of success through hard work. If a swarm of bees hovers around you without hurting you, you will be wealthy and respected, but if one stings you, a partner or colleague could prove untrustworthy. *See also* Beeswax, Sting.

Beeswax

Dreaming of beeswax is an indication that you could receive a sum of money, or that you will become rich through the inheritance of an unexpected legacy.

Beetle

To dream that black beetles creep down your back is a sign that you will be the subject of slander from someone whom you thought was your friend. If they creep over your face it means that you are the subject of praise from people with whom you have not previously had much connection. To dream that you kill beetles may indicate that you will shortly make active efforts to stop the slanderous rumours circulating about a friend of yours.

Beggar

A sudden change in your life is likely after a dream which features beggars, and possibly the need to be cautious when dealing with strangers, who may not all be as trustworthy as they appear.

Beheading

A classic dream of contrary, beheading is thought to indicate freedom from a pressing problem in your life, whatever that may be.

Bell

Dreaming of bells, especially if they are loud or discordant, suggests disturbance, arguments or radical change. This could relate to your personal life, a new career direction or problems at work. If the sound is a peel of small bells, it is more likely to relate to relationships between employer and employees. The circumstances can be turned to your advantage if you act with good judgement.

Bequest

To dream that you are bequeathing money or property to friends or relatives is a sure sign that you will soon receive money from an unexpected quarter. *See also* Will.

Betting

A dream in which you are placing bets should be taken as a warning to be more careful in your financial arrangements and certainly not to lend money to others.

Bicycle

A bicycle is symbolic of cyclical movement, ongoing but not necessarily finding the ultimate goal.

Bigamy

Another dream of contrary, this image is thought to indicate a happy and faithful relationship either with your current or a prospective partner.

Bird

The sound of birdsong in a dream indicates love, joy or good news, although the croaking of ravens or owls screeching indicates bad news. A flock of birds, especially if they are black, is supposed to indicate a loss of some kind, as is a bird or birds in a house. *See also* Bird of prey, Nest, individual birds

Bird of prey

Falcons, hawks or other birds of prey in a dream can have different meanings depending on the circumstances. If you are in control of the bird, it can indicate material gain, but if you feel threatened by the birds or if they attack you, it can be taken as a sign that other people may try to harm you or damage your reputation or progress. *See also* Bird

Bite

Traditionally, to dream you are bitten indicates that you will suffer from jealousy.

Black

Black is generally thought to be an unlucky colour in a dream, as it has connotations of unhappiness.

Blackbird

Hearing blackbirds singing is a positive symbol in a dream, although seeing blackbirds is generally thought to indicate problems and perhaps deceit. *See also* Bird.

Blindness

This can be a very distressing dream, but it is traditionally interpreted to suggest that you have put your trust in someone who does not have your best interests at heart. In the extreme, this might suggest that your employees lack loyalty, or your partner is unfaithful. For most people, however, it is an indication that they need to be more cautious in putting their confidence in others. *See also* Eye, Sight.

Blood

A dream in which you see blood, or someone bleeding, is generally thought to have negative implications. Since blood is essential to life, losing blood suggests that some kind of loss may follow, perhaps of affection, friends, money or possessions.

Blossom

Seeing a tree or shrub in full bloom in a dream is a potent symbol of joy and comfort. *See also* Tree.

Blue

Blue denotes happiness, prosperity and the respect of those close to you. *See also* Purple.

Boar

The image of a boar in a dream relates to powerful adversaries, so if you hunt or capture a wild boar, then you are likely to be successful, perhaps in business. If you are chased or injured, then you need to be more careful in your dealings with those in power. *See also* Animal.

Boat

Travelling in a boat on a river or lake is a calm dream suggesting prosperity and success, and perhaps moving in new, profitable directions. If the boat is adrift and you are lost, it suggests you should be thinking about firming up on your intentions and ambitions, or that you should avoid a dubious course of action you had been considering. If the boat is in danger of capsizing, you might find danger or problems ahead of you. *See also* individual boats.

Boil

If you see a boil somewhere on your body, it is an image suggesting minor ill health.

Bone

Seeing a quantity of bones in a dream is likely to suggest that you will have problems with the structure of your life which you will have to work hard to overcome. *See also* Skeleton.

Bonfire

To dream of helping to build a bonfire indicates that you might be about to undergo a fairly radical change of mind, discarding many opinions that you used to support, and vice versa. *See also* Fire, Flame.

Book

To dream of reading books, especially if you are surrounded by a considerable library, suggests that you may be more suited to a single life and may find your best creative outlets in the literary sphere. If you are reading the Bible, or other religious book, you are likely to be respected by a large circle of friends. To dream that your bookcase is almost empty of books is a sign that your talents are academic, although if your bookcase is filled with elegantly bound books in mint condition that have clearly never been read, then perhaps the opposite may be the case. *See also* Reading.

Borrowing

Borrowing something in a dream often indicates that you are not likely to have what you want.

Bottle

Full bottles are an indication that you are likely to get what you want; empty bottles signify a lack of something, perhaps health; bottles that have been knocked over are often thought to be an indication of problems or arguments at home.

Bouquet

Dreaming of carrying a bouquet has positive implications for relationships, but to throw one away suggest separation or relationship breakdowns. If you are presented with a beautiful bouquet in your dream, it is an indication of commitment. *See also* Flower.

Bow and arrow

Carrying a bow and arrow in a dream relates to desire or ambition. If you are shooting with the bow and arrow, your ambition is strong and likely to succeed.

Box

An empty box tends to be a predictor of unhappiness in love or relationship problems. If the box is full of useful articles, then you can expect the opposite.

Bracelet

If you dream that someone is fastening a bracelet on your wrist, it suggests a concern that they could have some unwarranted control over you.

Bramble

Being stuck in a patch of brambles, or trying to walk through them, means that you are likely to encounter many difficulties and delays. It can be a dream image indicating problems associated with unfair rumours or difficulties with relationships, either personal or professional. If you get through the brambles without being injured, then you should be able to find similar success in your waking life.

Brandy

A suggestion of good news is associated with a dream involving brandy.

Bread

Eating bread in a dream is generally a sign that you will have what you need to get through life. However, if you are forced to eat stale bread, or beg a crust from someone, this suggests that things may not be easy for you. Throwing away good bread is an indication that you could be wasting opportunities. *See also* Baker, Bakery.

Breakage

If you dream of breaking anything, it can indicate that something in your life is likely to be fractured or damaged in some way.

Breakfast

If you see yourself eating breakfast in your dream you should act carefully or be prepared to regret some of your actions.

Breasts

Dreaming about a woman's breasts relates to motherhood and your need for protection and nurturing.

Breath

Dreaming that you have bad breath indicates a fear that you are unpopular. If you have a genuine problem – even if only one of confidence – it can be overcome if you take the right, positive steps.

Bribe

For someone to dream that they receive a bribe is indicative of honesty of character.

Bride

To see a bride in a dream warns you to beware of a rival, either at work or in relationships.

Bridge

Crossing a bridge suggests that you will be successful, although standing under a bridge for any length of time is considered unlucky. To fall over on a bridge suggests that you may have problems in moving forward with a plan. If a bridge collapses while you are crossing it, you should review any major plans to ensure that they are well founded.

Brooch

A brooch is said to reflect artistic ability.

Broom

Dreaming of a broom can be taken as a warning to be cautious in your judgements of other people, especially if you are inclined to see the best in everyone. Someone may be trying to take advantage of you.

Brother

Dreaming about your brother indicates relationships with your family. Perhaps there is some uneasiness in family relationships that could be resolved with some careful thought and communication.

Bucket

To dream of a bucket with the bottom knocked out or with holes in it suggests that you could be the subject of fraudulent dealings and lose a lot if you are not careful. *See also* Tool.

Buckle

A belt buckle holds a belt together and as such it can be seen as an image of agreement or of the key to a particular aspect of life. Perhaps an important agreement will be broken, or a relationship fail.

Building

If you dream of a very tall building, it generally denotes long life and happiness. However, if you dream of building a house, or having one built, it can suggest that you will have to work hard in life and may not always achieve your objectives.

Bull

A bull symbolises an important person, so the significance of the dream can be found in how the bull reacts to you. *See also* Animal.

Bulldog

You are likely to renew acquaintance with old friends. *See also* Dog.

Burden

Carrying a burden in a dream suggests that you will depend upon others for help.

Burial

If you see yourself buried in a dream, you are likely to hear about some good luck, although if you are buried alive, it indicates prison or restraint. *See also* Coffin, Grave.

Butcher

Dreaming of a butcher is traditionally thought to relate to injury or disappointment.

Butterfly

To dream of a butterfly is a sign of inconstancy. *See also* Moth.

Cabinet

The dream image of a cabinet is suggestive of deceit or deception. Are you withholding something that could be harmful to yourself or someone else, or is someone in possession of knowledge that could be detrimental to you?

Cage

Seeing a cage in a dream suggests that you may be involved in a change of location, perhaps unexpectedly. If there is a bird in the cage, any changes will turn out for the best.

Cake

Baking cakes in a dream is an image of comfort and happiness. *See also* Baker, Baking.

Calendar

To dream that you are searching the calendar for a date you cannot find suggests that you are likely to have some important arrangements to make very shortly. If the dream ends before you find what you are looking for, expect change or cancellation.

Calm

A dream in which the overriding feeling is one of calm and relaxation suggests that any difficulties will be overcome and you are likely to be entering a period of happiness.

Camel

This extraordinary animal is suggestive of extraordinary events, changes or circumstances in your life.

Camera

If you are looking for a camera in your dream, be careful that someone is not trying to deceive you. If you are using a camera, the suggestion is that you want to focus more closely on events that are happening to you. Being filmed may indicate that you feel you are under scrutiny.

Can

A can is a sign of good news, especially if you see yourself drinking from the can.

Canal

To walk beside a muddy canal in your dream suggests that you will shortly experience problems either at home or at work. However, if the

Canary

Someone could be taking a positive interest in you if you dream of a canary, especially if it is singing. *See also* Bird.

Candle

To see a lighted candle is a dream image of good health, recovery if you are unwell, or an important event. If the candle is extinguished then a change of circumstances for the worse could be indicated. Dreaming that someone brings new candles into a room suggests the resolution of arguments is imminent.

Cannibalism

Cannibalism is a very startling image in a dream and is said to suggest that the ways you have chosen to advance yourself have involved, or could involve, injuring others. You are inclined to be too ruthless and it may be better to try to consider other people's feelings as well as your own.

Cannon

Hearing or seeing a cannon fired suggests that you should be on the lookout for problems in the near future as a result of some unexpected news. *See also* Gun.

Canoe

To paddle down a river in a canoe suggests that a friend will refuse your request for financial support. You are likely to have to cultivate self-reliance as your progress will be through your own efforts.

---

waters are clear and free flowing, you can look for happiness and success, even though you may have to work hard to achieve it. Falling into the canal suggests a sudden change of work or business arrangements.

Card

See Playing card.

Carpenter

A problem could threaten your equanimity, but it is likely to be resolved.

Carpet

New carpets are said to indicate financial outlay; while worn carpets mean success at work.

Carrot

Carrots are said to be a dream image of profit, particularly related to inheritance or unexpected legacy or windfall. *See also* Vegetable.

Carrying

To dream that you are carrying someone suggests profit and success, whereas if you are being carried it indicates a need for support.

Carving

Seeing carvings or someone carving in a dream highlights artistic ability, either in you or someone close to you. It is a very positive image.

Cashier

Other people are likely to try to transfer their problems to you if you dream that you are a cashier. Remain open and honest so that people judge you favourably.

Castle

Promotion and ambition are indicated by a dream set in a castle.

Castration

This is a dream relating to a fear of losing masculinity, sexual ability or an element of power.

Cat

A cat is an image of slyness or deceit and acts as a warning that you should be careful where you place your trust. If you kill a cat in a dream, then you are likely to wreak revenge on anyone who injures you. If the cat is restless, be wary of treacherous acquaintances. A cat washing itself suggests that you will command the respect and love of those close to you. *See also* Animal.

Caterpillar

Caterpillars are an unlucky image in a dream, suggesting bad luck or problems of which you cannot find the cause.

Cathedral

To attend a service in a cathedral suggests protection, happiness and the support of those around you. *See also* Church.

Cattle

A herd of healthy cattle denotes prosperity, and the successful outcome of a project. However, animals that are thin and undernourished have an opposite meaning.

Cauliflower

Dreaming that you are eating cauliflower indicates that you are likely to break any bad habits and feel much better for it. *See also* Vegetable.

Cave

Looking into a cave in a dream is thought to indicate changes in your life, as you are looking into the unknown.

Ceiling

A dream in which the ceiling of a room collapses on you suggests sudden change.

Cellar

To dream of being in a cellar traditionally suggests that you will have the opportunity to travel and make new contacts. If you are in a wine cellar, at least one of those new acquaintances could be duplicitous.

Cemetery

If your dream takes place in a cemetery, it is generally thought to suggest that you will find a way to solve problems.

Centipede

A centipede is a symbol of bad luck, which might come from unexpected quarters.

Chain

To dream of a chain with long links is an image of communication. If the chain is unbroken, then this augurs well for your dealings with others, whereas if it is broken, it suggests that it might be advisable to apply more thought and care to your dealings with others.

Chair

Sitting beside an empty chair in a dream suggests that you are hoping to meet someone who will be influential in your life, or get together again with someone you have not seen for some time.

Champagne

Being drunk on champagne is a traditional warning to take care of those with whom you associate. *See also* Wine.

Change

If an atmosphere of change is the underlying feeling in your dream, it suggests a period of unrest, although this will turn out well if you dream that you benefited from the change.

Charade

To act in a charade at a party is a sign that you may not receive many social invitations for a while as your friends seek to avoid you. Try to find out the cause of the problem and resolve it.

Charcoal

If you dream that you are sitting beside a fire of charcoal you will soon hear exciting news from friends abroad.

Charity

If you are asked to give to a charity in your dream and you give generously, this is a sign of joy, although if you refuse to give it is a suggestion that a change in your attitude to life would be beneficial.

Cheating

To be cheated at a game of chance, or in any purchase, suggests that you will be a good judge of character and circumspect in your dealings, and will benefit from that.

Cheese

To eat cheese in a dream is an image suggesting profit or advantage. *See also* Eating.

Cheque

Dreaming about receiving a cheque is not as good as it might at first appear, as it indicates that you may not be able to trust everyone around you. Be sure about people before you place your trust in them, as it could be that someone fairly close to you is a hypocrite or an impostor.

Cherry

Enjoying fresh, ripe cherries is generally a positive dream image, but if you eat too many cherries in a dream, especially if they are out of season, they are a symbol of disappointment and even rejection in love. *See also* Fruit.

Chess

The game of chess is symbolic of confrontation or perhaps difficult negotiations. Is someone you are dealing with trying to test you, or trying to mislead you? *See also* Backgammon, Draughts, Game.

Chestnut

A chestnut – whether a sweet chestnut or a horse chestnut – is a fruit that is heavily armoured and protected. If you dream that you are collecting or seeing chestnuts, it could be that something is getting in the way of what you want or has value to you. It is not necessarily something physical; it could be a relationship, a promotion, the resolution of an argument. Try to define that barrier and you are more likely to be able to overcome it. If you are eating and enjoying sweet chestnuts, this is a positive sign that difficulties will be overcome, or barriers removed. *See also* Nut.

Chicken

Dreaming of chickens in a farmyard usually relates to your home life. If they are running about in a random fashion, you may have minor problems. If they are strutting, the difficulties could be more severe. If they run away, a loss is indicated. However, if they are feeding quietly, you can be reassured of some good times ahead. *See also* Cock.

Child

Children in a dream are generally considered a positive image, especially if they are happy and playing contentedly.

Childbirth

If a woman dreams she has given birth to a child without being pregnant, it is a sign that she will accomplish her ambitions. In general, dreaming of childbirth is an indication of success, perhaps through hard work, realisation of intentions and new beginnings. It is a very potent image in a dream.

Chocolate

A dream involving buying chocolate is a warning to be wary of a thoughtless or frivolous action. If you are being given or are eating chocolate, however, you could receive a gift from someone unexpected.

Choir

Hearing a choir sing suggests communication, although if the music is dreary or discordant, be careful that the person you are speaking with actually means what they say. If you are singing in the choir, you should be proud of your communication skills and try to develop your abilities.

Choking

A feeling that you are choking can be a very frightening dream image. It relates to a communication-based conflict. Perhaps you want to tell someone something but feel it would be unwise, or you are worried that you are not able to communicate something as effectively as you would like.

Christ

To talk with Jesus Christ in a dream signifies consolation.

Christening

A christening is an image of welcome, belonging and new life, although changes may not necessarily be straightforward or easy.

Christmas

Images of Christmas in a dream are connected with reconciliation or reunion with old friends.

Christmas tree

Christmas is a time of celebration, and dreaming of a beautifully decorated Christmas tree suggests that the next Christmas will be a memorable one.

Church

Seeing yourself praying in a church is an image of comfort and contentment, but if you are behaving in an inappropriate way for a holy place, it can indicate that there is envy either in your attitude or that of those around you. *See also* Cathedral.

Churchyard

To dream of walking in a churchyard suggests you may experience a pleasant surprise, with a possibility of an improvement in your finances.

Cider

Cider, especially if you are drinking it, is an indicator of good luck with particular relevance to work or education.

Cigar

To dream that you are enjoying smoking a first-class cigar suggests that you will find ways to relax and release the stresses that might otherwise be considerable.

Circus

Consider carefully whether you are becoming too selfish or developing other bad habits if you dream of a circus. It will be to your advantage to improve your behaviour. *See also* Clown.

Cliff

Standing looking over the edge of a cliff highlights a risk that has to be taken, or an important decision that has to be made. It underlines both your uncertainty about what you have to face and the importance of taking that step into the unknown future.

Climbing

Climbing is a sign of ambition and striving for authority and power. If you reach the top of whatever you are climbing, then your prospects are good. *See also* Ladder, Mountain, Tree.

Clock

Hearing or seeing a clock in a dream indicates that you are trying hard to improve your circumstances. If the clock has stopped or is broken, it suggests illness or difficulty.

Clothes

What you are wearing in a dream can be taken to give an indication of your general circumstances and both how you perceive yourself and how others see you. If you are smartly dressed, things should go well for you; you have a positive self-image and others also regard you well. However, if you recognise that you are seriously overdressed, then think about whether you are being too extravagant either in the way you behave or in your opinion of yourself. If you are shabbily dressed, you may be unsuccessful, feeling negative about yourself, or feeling that others are putting you down or holding you in contempt; perhaps you would benefit from being more forthcoming. If you are embarrassed in your dream because you are scantily dressed, then you are likely to be feeling anxious about something.

Buying new clothes suggests good things to come. Putting on new clothes indicates a possible change of circumstances, perhaps marriage, a new relationship or a new job. Seeing your clothes damaged or destroyed is not a good sign, as it suggests an attack on you or your reputation.

Colours can also be significant, so if there is a predominance of one colour in your clothing, this can add to the potential meaning of the dream. White is a positive colour, while black has negative implications. Yellow suggests suspicion or jealousy. Blue indicates happiness. Red suggests news, especially from a long way away. Multi-coloured clothes indicate variety in life. *See also* individual items of clothing and fabric.

Cloud

A cloudy sky, or clouds passing across the sun, suggests problems in your relationships, and the nature of the problems can be indicated by the type of cloud. Heavier or more slow-moving clouds indicate more serious problems. Light, swiftly moving clouds generally show that you will only suffer minor problems. *See also* Sky.

Clove

Seeing cloves indicates that your children will be a source of great pleasure to you.

Clover

Walking in a field of clover suggests health, wealth and happiness. *See also* Flower.

Clown

A clown may be a warning to be careful not to give the impression that you are stupid. *See also* Circus.

Coat

A coat is a symbol of the most important element in how you view yourself and how others see you. *See also* Clothes.

Cock

To dream you see or hear a cock crow is an image suggesting happiness or good news. Seeing cocks fighting suggests arguments or disagreements. *See also* Chicken.

Cocoa

To dream that you are drinking cocoa, hot chocolate or any other warm and comforting drink is a very good indication that you will be contented and relaxed. *See also* Drink.

Coffee

Drinking coffee in a dream suggests that you need something to wake you up and make you more aware of dealing properly with others, especially at work. *See also* Drink.

Coffin

Dreaming of a coffin is generally thought to be an indication of problems or loss, and getting used to the fact that change, or even death, are part of life's experience. *See also* Burial, Funeral.

Coin

Piles of coins in a dream are suggestive of financial gain, although if you see them but cannot obtain them, you may find financial success eludes you. *See also* Money.

Cold

If you feel that you are suffering from a cold in a dream, it may be that changes are happening in your relationships with someone close to you. Think about what you want from the relationship and act accordingly, but remember to be sympathetic to the needs of others.

Collar bone

If you dream that you have broken your collar bone in an accident, it suggests a possible accident or problem among your circle of friends. *See also* Bone.

Combing

Combing hair suggests comforting and smoothing of difficulties. You may have to undergo a difficult phase but you will have the support and intelligence you need to get through any problems. *See also* Hair.

Comet

A comet is traditionally an image of problems.

Communion

If you dream of taking communion, it suggests happiness, enjoyment and love.

Compasses

Some of those who are studying with you could be progressing at a faster pace and you might do well to apply yourself more assiduously.

Concert

To dream of taking part in a successful concert suggests that you could play an important part in society or work well with your friends and colleagues. However, if the music is discordant or badly played, you are more likely to be spiteful and could make yourself unpopular if you do not change your behaviour. *See also* Music.

Confrontation

To dream that you confront someone who has deceived you is a sign that you will not have courage to speak in your own defence when opposed by someone who does not believe or practise some of the principles which you adopt.

Confusion

Dreaming that things around you are in confusion is a sign that your present plans need to be organised if you are not to waste your time and energy.

Congregation

To dream that you see or are part of a large congregation assembled in a church or place of worship is a sign that you must be careful with your friendships. There is a possibility that you will be left alone when you need help or support, although this may not be through any fault of your own.

Conjurer

A conjurer uses sleight of hand to deceive, and this dream suggests that someone is also trying to deceive you. *See also* Magic.

Constipation

Are you trying to hold on to something that you should really let go?

Conversation

Having a conversation with people you know to be important or influential suggests that you will find the means for improvement in your life. If you are talking with your brother or sister, you could be anxious about something and might do well to communicate your anxieties to others; they may be able to reassure you more easily than you thought. Chatting idly when you are meant to be paying attention suggests envy, either in yourself or in others towards you.

Cooking

To dream you are cooking suggests new relationships.

Corkscrew

To dream of using a corkscrew is indicative of illness, but not necessarily your own. If the cork breaks, the problem could be a serious one.

Corn

Gathering ripe corn is a positive dream image of profit and plenty, although a field of corn damaged by bad weather or gathering diseased corn both indicate the opposite.

Corpse

Seeing a corpse in a dream suggests that you must think carefully before entering into any agreements or serious relationships. *See also* Death.

Countryside

Dreaming that you are in the countryside is an indication that you will succeed in your latest project if you apply yourself to it seriously.

Court case

To dream that you have been involved in a court case and convicted of a crime is a sign that you are a law-abiding person and should continue to follow your conscience. *See also* Judge, Magistrate, Law, Lawyer.

Cousin

To dream that you have received a communication from your cousin or a similar relative is a suggestion that you may receive news from an old lover who may want to renew the relationship.

Cow

To dream you see or have many cows signifies wealth and plenty directly related to the number of animals in the herd. *See also* Animal.

Cowslip

A sudden and unexpected change in your circumstances is suggested by a dream of cowslips in full bloom. *See also* Flower.

Cradle

A broken or empty cradle is associated with illness.

Crane

Seeing a flock of cranes flying across the sky suggests difficulties on the horizon. *See also* Bird.

Crawling

To dream that you are crawling on the floor is a bad omen indicating a downturn in your fortunes, although it should only be temporary if you handle the situation correctly.

Cricket

If you see a cricket or hear it chirp, be wary of a stranger's flattery.

Crocodile

An awareness of false friends is suggested by this image in a dream. *See also* Animal.

Crocus

Happiness at home is suggested by dreaming of crocuses in flower. *See also* Flower.

Cross

A cross of gold suggests happy relationships with no shortage of material advantages, while a wooden cross indicates happy relationships, although not necessarily financially profitable ones. Seeing yourself carrying a cross is an indication of worries and responsibilities. Perhaps you can find ways to share those responsibilities in order to lighten your load.

Crossroads

Standing at a crossroads is an easy dream to interpret as it emerges from your own feelings that you have decisions to make and are confused as to which way to go. Pursue the metaphor: find a map, decide on where you want to finish your journey, and then you should be able to see which road to take to reach your destination.

Crow

Crows or other similar birds in a dream are generally indicative of anger or loss. *See also* Bird, Raven, Rook.

Crowd

Being in a crowd is indicative of how you relate to other people and possibly how you tend either to take the lead or try to avoid responsibility in a group situation.

Crown

A potent image of authority, carrying or wearing a crown suggests that you are well respected.

Crutch

To dream you are walking on crutches, or seeing someone else walking on crutches, suggests that you could encounter a problem that will require the support of others to help you through.

Cry

To hear someone cry out in a dream suggests that you could receive unexpected news.

Crying

If you see yourself crying in a dream, it is a dream of contrary indicating that you will soon have a good reason to feel very happy.

Cuckoo

A cuckoo in a dream is an indication that you must be careful of the choices you make, especially with regard to relationships. *See also* Bird.

Cul-de-sac

Reaching a dead end is exactly how you are feeling at the present time. You may have to retrace your steps or find another route, but certainly repeating the same patterns of behaviour is not likely to be successful.

Cup

A full cup suggests opportunities that you should grasp without hesitation if you want to be successful, while an empty cup is a sign of troubled times ahead.

Cupboard

To dream of a well-stocked kitchen cupboard or larder suggests that you can expect a time of happiness ahead as you have laid the foundations for things to turn out well for you.

Curtain

A curtain in a dream is an image suggesting that something is being hidden from you, or that you need more information on which to base an important decision. If you touch or pull back the curtain, you will soon discover what you need to know.

Cypress tree

Although dreaming of trees often has positive implications, cypress trees are generally considered to indicate problems. *See also* Tree.

Dagger

To dream of seeing a dagger, either held by yourself or someone else, suggests feelings of aggression, perhaps that you want to cut something out of your life. It could indicate a serious argument with a close acquaintance with long-term consequences. If you are attacked in the dream, then you may be feeling vulnerable.

Dahlia

A dahlia indicates thrift and financial stability. *See also* Flower.

Daisy

A daisy is a dream image of openness and trust. If you dream that you are gathering daisies, it suggests that you will be lucky and can expect to gain what you want in life, although you should be wary of being over-trusting of those whom you do not know. *See also* Flower.

Damson

Fresh fruit in season is a positive dream image, but out of season it suggests that some aspect of your life could become complicated and difficult. *See also* Fruit.

Dancing

Dancing is a symbol of freedom and is spiritually uplifting. It is a positive dream image and often suggests a high intensity of emotion on a subject close to your heart. *See also* Ball.

Dandelion

Images of dandelions in dreams often relate to relationships. If you see a profusion of these yellow flowers, it is a good sign of positive friendships. *See also* Flower.

Danger

To dream of being in danger suggests that you are likely to be successful in life; whereas to dream that you avoid danger can indicate that you might be more successful if you took some calculated risks.

Darkness

Darkness is a symbol of disappointment, especially if the space is confined and the atmosphere negative, but if you manage to find your way out of the dark place, then it becomes a more favourable image. If you are groping about in the dark and unable to orientate yourself, then you could have decisions to make about a partner or something important that are causing you some disquiet. Collect together the facts of the situation before you try to make a decision.

Dawn

To watch the dawn breaking in a dream indicates forthcoming change as it represents new beginnings or perhaps a new understanding of existing circumstances. You may find that you are able to look at things in a different light and discover new solutions.

Deafness

If you dream that you are deaf, the dream suggests that someone may protect you from hearing or finding out about something that would distress you, or perhaps that you have the capacity to avoid a problem if you make the right choices.

Death

Dreams involving death are generally not as disturbing as it might at first appear because of the effect of the dream state and the fact that the traditional image of death is taken to mean the end of one phase but the beginning of another. Dreaming that you are dead can therefore be taken as a token of change, often progress, in some sphere of your life; if you see someone else and believe them to be dead, then the change may affect them directly, or they could be taken as the instrument of change in your life. You may soon find a new job, start a new relationship, be about to marry or have children. *See also* Corpse, Funeral, Hearse.

Debate

To dream that you are involved in a debate on a serious subject is indicative of financial profit or business success.

Debt

To pay a debt in a dream denotes that you are likely to lose some money through your own carelessness. If you dream that someone is repaying a debt to you, be very wary of lending money to anyone. *See also* Bailiff.

Decorating

Dreaming that you are painting or decorating is often thought to suggest that you may have to resort to your skills in making things good, as you could be in for a lean time.

Deer

Seeing a running deer in a dream underlines the fact that you should take more advantage of your physical, perhaps sporting skills. If you chase the deer, with little or no hope of catching it, beware of wasting your time on projects that, deep down, you know cannot be successful. To kill a deer is traditionally thought to indicate that you are likely either to be the winner in an argument or altercation, or gain something unexpectedly from someone you either did not know or did not like. *See also* Animal, Stag, Venison.

Delight

If the overwhelming feeling in a dream is that you are delighted with an event in your life, it can suggest bad news or a problem arising from an unexpected source.

Dentist

Dreaming of visiting a dentist is often thought to suggest that you need to take more care of yourself, particularly from a health point of view.

Desert

To dream that you are travelling in the desert indicates you may encounter difficulties and dangers.

Desk

Important news is likely to follow a dream in which you see yourself sitting at a desk, especially if you are near to a window. If you see a stranger sitting at a desk, especially if you recognise it as your own desk, there may be legal issues to deal with before very long.

Despair

An atmosphere of despair in a dream is often very disturbing but can be cathartic, purging feelings that you are overwhelmed with responsibilities. It is often thought to suggest that you are moving on to another phase and that things will improve.

Destruction

Destroying something in a dream suggests that you should be careful not instantly to say what first comes into your head without thinking about the consequences. You will not necessarily create the impression that you would like, and other people could drag you into difficult issues if you are not more cautious.

Devil

The devil can manifest in many forms in dreams, depending on your personal attitude, but the important factor is that you recognise him to be the epitome of evil, symbolising deceit and treachery. How this could appear in your life usually relates to the situation in the dream, and this could also give you an indication of how you can avoid finding yourself in such circumstances. If you are captured by the devil, you could find that the feeling of relief on waking is so intense that it inspires you to a change of direction.

Dew

To dream of the dew glittering in the morning sun is a very lucky omen, indicating encouragement, happiness, wealth and success. In general, what you most want to achieve will be within your grasp.

Diamond

Diamonds belonging to someone else suggest profit and success; if they belong to you, then that success is only likely to be yours if you are more careful with your money. If you are seen to be eating diamonds, that is a sign of potential success. Sparkling diamonds generally indicate happiness. *See also* Jewel.

Dice

You could be in danger of losing your money, or something valuable, following a dream of playing at dice as the image is one of deceit.

Difficulty

Many dreams go by contrary, and believing that you are in some difficulty in your dream is usually a favourable sign for improvement or progress.

Digging

Digging in fertile soil is generally thought to be an image suggesting that you will find something valuable if you look in the right place. It may not mean anything material, but could be a new relationship, a promotion or anything beneficial. *See also* Gardening, Treasure.

Dinner

Dreaming that you are dining alone at a table set for several people suggests that you will have problems to solve, but should be able to do so successfully.

Dinner party

Being present at a dinner party suggests that you could be about to suffer the consequences of misplaced trust. If someone is referring to a piece of paper, then the issue could relate to money. If someone is making a speech, take care that you do not fall victim to flattery; not everyone means what they say, or says what they mean.

Dirt

Filth and dirt in a dream suggest malice.

Discussion

You are likely to make a success of life by your individual efforts rather than from anyone's help if you dream of being involved in a discussion with several people. To have a friendly discussion with an acquaintance suggests promotion opportunities at work, or an improvement in the affairs of your partner. *See also* Argument, Quarrel.

Disgrace

Feeling that you are in disgrace because of a thoughtless action suggests that you are capable of displaying a tact that will gain you the respect of your colleagues and friends.

Disguise

Disguise in a dream is an image suggesting confusion or lack of recognition. You may meet up with old friends but fail to recognise them, or be mistaken in your assessment of a new friend or colleague.

Distress

Great distress suggests that you could become indebted to someone.

Distrust

If someone appears to distrust you in a dream, it could be that your friends have been talking about you behind your back. You should perhaps take steps to ensure that you will not have cause to regret ever having known one or more of them. To dream that you have reason to distrust a person generally indicates bad luck for you or someone close to you.

Ditch

Falling into a ditch indicates loss, accident or legal problems.

Diving

Diving into deep water in a dream suggests exactly the same as the common expression: you could be involved in something risky by placing your trust in someone who is not worthy of it, or in some other way find yourself in a difficult situation.

Doctor

A doctor is a positive dream image related to someone who may be a healer or an authority figure of some kind. The dream usually indicates good health and good luck.

Dog

Friendly dogs, or dogs that belong to you, symbolise fidelity, courage and affection, whereas if they are aggressive, they indicate enemies. Dogs barking are an indication of potential arguments but they are likely to be resolved in your favour. A dog baying at the moon suggests that you may be asked to help someone. *See also* individual dogs.

Dolphin

Although dolphins are friendly and beautiful creatures, as a traditional dream image they are said to be trying to bring you a friendly warning that you should change your habits or make some other changes to your life in order to be happy.

Donkey

As a dream image, a donkey indicates someone who is stubborn and unintelligent, although this does not necessarily refer to you. Perhaps someone at work is being obstructive or looking for an argument. Try to be patient and communicate clearly, but don't lower your standards or expectations. *See also* Animal.

Door

An unexpectedly open door in a dream should alert you to be aware of potential opportunities that could be beneficial to you. If you are surrounded by open doors and do not know which way to turn, you have a difficult decision to make; accumulate as much information as you can before you commit yourself. To be knocking at a door and be invited into a house suggests new contacts, but if the door is not opened, you could be in for a disappointment. If you are hanging around the back door of a house trying to get in and not succeeding, there are likely to be moves ahead.

Dove

A dove is an omen of good luck and can suggest a happily married life or a successful business. If doves are feeding from your hand, it relates to travel or moves of some kind. *See also* Bird.

Dragon

A dragon in a dream generally relates to authority, power or wealth, and you can base your interpretations on how the image appears in the dream and how that relates to your circumstances.

Dragonfly

The dragonfly has a fragile beauty that suggests freedom but also that freedom can be oppressed or undermined by many factors in life, although it is nonetheless valuable.

Draughts

Playing draughts suggests that someone could be trifling with you. Try to be more astute in your assessment of other people. *See also* Backgammon, Chess, Game.

Dress

To spend money on an expensive and beautiful dress suggests that this will not be possible for you in your waking life, and that you may have to practise economy. However, if you dream that your dress is torn and that you have repaired it, you may never be rich but you are unlikely to want for the necessities in life.

Drink

To dream that you are thirsty and that someone offers you a drink suggests that you will meet a few friends or make a discovery that will be of benefit to you. *See also* Drunkenness, Thirst, individual drinks.

Driving

If you have a dream in which you are driving a car, it suggests that you may have acquired a habit that could lead you into trouble.

Drowning

Images of drowning in a dream, whether seeing yourself or another person drowning, are considered images of contrary, in that they tend to suggest that you may encounter difficulties but that you will overcome them. *See also* Sea, Shipwreck, Water.

Drum

A drum in a dream is generally considered a symbol of fame, especially if it is being played loudly. *See also* Music.

Drunkenness

Something of which you presently know nothing will soon come to your attention and could be advantageous to you, although if you are so drunk that you vomit, you could be in danger of wasting the opportunities you are offered. *See also* Drink.

Duck

Ducks swimming suggests that you will glide over any problems you encounter. Flying ducks suggests good news. *See also* Bird.

Duet

To dream you sing a duet with someone of the opposite sex suggests that you may find the partner you want. However, if they are of the same sex, it is more likely that you will encounter rivals at work.

Eagle

To dream that an eagle flies over your head signifies achievement or fame, although if you see an eagle on its nest, it could indicate that you are being too lazy to achieve what you have set out to do. *See also* Bird.

Ear

Dreaming that you have many ears indicates that you will be popular with friends or employees. If your ears are larger than usual, you will be helped by those you take into your confidence. However, if your ear is injured or painful, you could be offended or insulted by someone to whom you have entrusted a confidential piece of information. If your ear has been cut off, it is an image of lost friendships.

Earring

Receiving a present of earrings suggests that someone is trying to befriend you, but you might not necessarily feel as strongly for them. If you are giving the present, then the reverse could be the case.

Earthquake

Experiencing an earthquake in a dream is a very vivid image of radical and unexpected change, especially on an emotional level. You may be feeling insecure about your current circumstances and worried about the unknown, but the more realistic you can be about the possibilities open to you, the more likely you are to be able to turn them to your advantage. Sometimes changes forced upon us by circumstances can turn out to be major life opportunities.

Earthworm

A dream about earthworms suggests insidious enemies.

Earwig

If you dream of earwigs, it suggests you could be pestered by gossip. It may be advantageous to find out who is spreading unkind rumours and put a stop to it.

Easel

Buying or using an easel is a symbol of creativity, perhaps a creative skill, perhaps something involving children – perhaps even the creation of wealth.

Easter

Easter is a happy time related to new life, and this image generally suggests an introduction that will be advantageous to you or bring happiness in some way.

Eating

Dreaming of eating suggests loss, although watching other people eating indicates that the problem could relate to someone close to you. *See also* Feasting, Meal, individual foods.

Eavesdropping

To dream that you eavesdrop on a private conversation is a sign of approaching problems, possibly caused by unscrupulous people who show no concern for the consequences of their actions.

Echo

To hear an echo in your dream is an image suggesting that you could accidentally hear something that could be valuable to you, perhaps a business secret, perhaps the fact that someone of whom you have secretly been fond could return your affection.

Eclipse

An eclipse of the Moon is an image of loss relating to a woman. *See also* Moon.

Egg

An egg is a traditional symbol of life, so collecting or seeing eggs suggests advantages in life or new beginnings. If they are broken, it is an indication of lost opportunities.

Elbow

To dream of a pain in, or any trouble with, your elbow may be taken as a sign that you will have need of all your strength in an emergency which will soon arise.

Elderberry

Elderberries are traditionally thought to be an image representing potential trouble in relationships, or even illness. *See also* Fruit.

Elephant

A single elephant in a dream suggests stability in love and domestic happiness. Giving an elephant something to eat or drink indicates that you could be indebted to a powerful person, or support them to your advantage. A herd of elephants suggests that you could experience a major surprise. *See also* Animal.

Elm

To dream of a tall elm tree is an omen that either you or perhaps your partner may rise to distinction through application of intelligence. *See also* Tree.

Elopement

Dreaming that you elope with a stranger suggests an unexpected and early marriage, or perhaps a new relationship. Eloping with your partner can indicate a potential problem in the early stages of your relationship.

Embrace

Embracing someone in a dream is a sign of existing closeness, but also of potential separation.

Embroidery

To dream of embroidery suggests that your affection is returned. *See also* Sewing.

Emerald

An emerald is a symbol of annoyance, rivalry or jealousy. *See also* Jewel.

Employment

If you are looking for a job in a dream but cannot find one, it suggests that you will be loyal to your employer for many years. If you do find employment in your dream, you may soon be looking for a new job.

Enchantment

To dream you are enchanted signifies secrets and sorrows.

Enemy

To dream you are obstructed by an adversary signifies success in business, although if you are talking with them, it indicates that you should be cautious in your dealings and make sure you can trust those around you.

Engagement

To dream that you become engaged to be married is a suggestion that you are unlikely to be married for some time. A business engagement indicates that you may have problems at work, especially if the other person does not arrive. An engagement with a friend suggests quarrels or disagreements, perhaps as the result of a misunderstanding.

Engraving

To dream that you are engraving your name on metal denotes that you will have an offer of good, regular work at a new company.

Enjoyment

Enjoying yourself in a dream suggests something disagreeable may soon happen: perhaps an argument, perhaps an unwanted journey, perhaps a work-related problem.

Envelope

Envelopes are a symbol of communication, related to receiving, or not receiving, letters or other messages.

Envy

If you are envied in a dream you are likely to be admired in life.

Epaulet

Seeing someone wearing epaulets on his or her coat is an image of promotion or advancement.

Escape

Anxiety is usually represented by a dream in which you are trying to escape. Inability to escape indicates trouble will overtake you; a successful escape means you should find the strength and intelligence to overcome your present difficulties.

Estate

To dream that you are the owner of considerable estates relates to your potential partners. An indication of the character of your partner and your future life can be gleaned from the nature of your land in the dream. *See also* Field.

Evening

The fading light of the evening suggests relaxation and calm, perhaps also a maturity of outlook.

Evergreen

Evergreens in profusion, either plants or branches cut for decoration, suggest good luck, success and happiness throughout the year. It is a very positive dream image. If you pick them, you are likely to have the true friendship of someone. *See also* Tree.

Examination

To dream of passing an examination with consummate ease is not necessarily a good sign, whereas if you appear to be having problems with an exam, you are more likely to be preparing wisely for tests in your waking life.

Exchange

Seeing yourself exchanging goods with someone in a dream is an indication that you should be more careful in how you do business or in where you place your trust. There is potential for you to be swindled if you are not more cautious.

Excrement

Relieving yourself in public suggests that things could come to light that would perhaps better remain hidden.

Execution

Watching an execution of a criminal is traditionally thought to suggest that the negative influences in your life should be minimal, or that some change, or even loss, should eventually turn out to be to your benefit.

Executor

To dream that you are the executor of a will of someone who has recently died suggests that you may have to stand surety for someone, or in some way be a guarantor for a friend or colleague. *See also* Bequest, Will.

Exercise

To dream that you are taking vigorous exercise is a sign that hard work is to follow.

Exhaustion

If you dream that you are exhausted after violent exercise, it suggests a change in your attitude is likely to be necessary, so that you become more used to hard work and responsibility.

Exhibition

Visiting an exhibition in a dream suggests that your inclinations tend more towards indoor rather than outdoor pursuits.

Exile

Experiencing a dream that you have become an exile in a foreign country suggests a very strong connection with your own country or locality. You may expect to deepen your local roots, or find a way to support your local community in some way.

Explosion

An explosion suggests a huge release of energy, which could relate to anger, sorrow, or any other deeply felt emotions. In the aftermath of an explosion, there could be room for new understanding if old feelings have been pushed away.

Eye

The eyes are the windows of the soul and the Ancients viewed them as representing faith, the will and the light of understanding. Therefore dreaming that you have beautiful eyes and sharp eyesight is a very positive image, while if your eyes are injured or your sight poor, it suggests loss of faith, self-esteem or spiritual direction. *See also* Blindness, Sight.

Eyebrow

Eyebrows and eyelids are generally thought to be symbolic of the respect of others, so if they are prominent, you can deduce that you are well regarded by those around you, or if they are insignificant, perhaps you could do more to command the appreciation of others.

Face

A beautiful face is a dream image suggesting sound reputation. To dream you wash your face suggests that you regret something you have done and want to find a way to make amends for a mistake. To see a strange face is an indication that you may soon be making either a permanent or a temporary change in your life, perhaps of location. To see your own face, or any other beautiful face, reflected in a mirror is a suggestion of a long life. A group of familiar faces suggests an invitation to a happy event.

Factory

Change or accident is indicated by seeing yourself working in a factory.

Failure

To dream that you fail in anything indicates that you are likely to succeed through your own efforts.

Fainting

If you see yourself fainting in a dream, it suggests that circumstances related to trust could occur in your life. It may be that someone you have trusted lets you down, or that your trust is betrayed, for example by being robbed.

Fair

Jealousy or deception is indicated by dreaming about attending a fair or similar event.

Fairy

The significance of the image of fairies or other sprites in a dream varies depending on their appearance in the dream. They can be either helpful or mischievous, depending on their character and the circumstances in the dream.

Falling

Not surprisingly, images of falling are suggestive of sudden and undesirable change. Falling from a tree often relates to changing your job. Falling into mud or dirt indicates that someone may want you to fail. *See also* Hole, Precipice.

Fame

Dreaming that you have suddenly shot to fame suggests that you could need to be more cautious and take a longer-term view, perhaps start saving more regularly, so that you can cope with events more smoothly rather than finding life is a struggle.

Famine

A dream of famine suggests the opposite: prosperity, health and happiness. *See also* Hunger.

Farewell

To dream of saying goodbye to a friend who is about to leave you for good is a sign that you should never have cause to doubt them. If you are the one who is leaving, you should have the opportunity to make new friends.

Farm

Being on a farm suggests family quarrels, although if you are working on the farm, then there is likely to be a steady improvement in your affairs, even if they don't start out too well.

Fasting

To dream that you spend a day without eating suggests that you should receive something that you need.

Fat

Being fat but healthy in a dream is a sign that you have the potential to be rich and to make a success of your life. As long as you are not also ill in the dream, this is a very good omen.

Father

Seeing your father in a dream is traditionally thought to underline his love for you and that he should always be there to support you.

Fear

If you experience an overwhelming feeling of fear at something that is happening in your dream, it is an indication of considerable happiness in store for you. It could relate to money, a successful business deal, the fact that your partner, family or children gain a good job or you might receive some excellent news. To dream that you are frightened without knowing the reason suggests that you can afford to be less anxious about other people's behaviour.

Feasting

To dream you are at a feast suggests that you should prepare yourself to meet disappointments, particularly concerning the thing you are most anxious about. If you plan carefully and try to take the longer-term view, you may be able to mitigate or even avoid the potential problems. *See also* Eating.

Feather

Seeing feathers floating in the air is an image suggesting a coming anxiety that may be difficult to understand or to solve.

Feeding animals

To dream you are feeding cattle, horses, poultry or pigs indicates that you should be successful at work and have enough to support your dependants. *See also* Animal.

Fence

Building a fence is a symbol of success through hard work unless, of course, it falls down. Climbing a fence indicates a sudden rise in life; creeping under a fence is a warning to avoid shady transactions.

Fern

A luxuriant growth of ferns in a dream is a sign of good luck, although if their growth is stunted or they are diseased, you are likely to encounter difficulties, perhaps through disappointment with your children. *See also* Plant.

Ferret

A ferret in your dream is a sign that you have an intense curiosity and are driven to search out difficult things, explain problems, unravel mysteries and understand puzzles. *See also* Animal.

Festival

To dream that you are at a festival or celebration is an image suggesting that you may soon experience something that could cause you distress.

Fever

Experiencing a fever in a dream is generally an indication of an overriding preoccupation with something. Would you benefit from taking a more objective view?

Field

Wandering in extensive open fields often suggests that your life has become monotonous and would benefit from an injection of imagination or change, although if the fields are planted with healthy crops, then the likelihood that you will succeed in your endeavours is high. If the field is ploughed, hard work could be involved, but that is not necessarily a bad thing. *See also* Estate.

Fig

To dream you see figs in season signifies joy, pleasure and realising your ambitions; you are unlikely to have to do without the things you really need. Out of season, they indicate the opposite. *See also* Fruit.

Fighting

Fighting is an ominous symbol in a dream that traditionally suggests problems of some kind. They may be related to a loss, an argument, your health, problems at work or in your relationships.

Find

Finding something, either by accident or because you have been looking for it, suggests that you are likely to succeed at work, although perhaps not so well in relationships. If you find a purse, make sure your savings are safe and that you are paying enough attention to managing your budget. If you find a piece of jewellery, work harder at cementing your relationships.

Finger

Fingers are thought to represent people close to you, especially if they are dependent on you, such as children or employees, so if your fingers are large and healthy-looking, then you are well regarded by such people. To injure or burn your fingers, however, suggests envy or lack of respect. If you grow an extra finger, you might expect to meet new people, have a child or expand your business.

Fingernail

Long fingernails suggest profit, possibly augmented by someone close to you, perhaps a dependent, and the opposite suggest unhappiness and loss. Biting your nails is suggestive of arguments and frustration.

Fire

A cosy fire in a fireplace is a positive sign that everything is going well with you. If you see a fire burning elsewhere, it suggests a change of circumstances. Burning your fingers suggests envy, but if you handle fire without getting burned, you are likely to achieve your ambitions, although your path may not necessarily be without incident. Seeing someone holding a burning torch suggests that any attempts to hide underhand dealings may be unsuccessful. Seeing a house on fire without being destroyed indicates good fortune, but if it is destroyed, this indicates the opposite. If the fire is located in a particular room, the dream suggests problems related to the person most closely associated with that room. If you see your bed on fire, it suggests difficulties with relationships. *See also* Bonfire, Flame, Smoke.

Fireside

To dream of sitting by the fireside with someone you love is a clear image of a contented and happy life.

Firework

Fireworks in a dream suggest bad temper, arguments, frustration and anger. You should be particularly careful not to be deceived by appearances, and try not to lose your temper. You will always put yourself in a more advantageous position if you remain cool and logical; if you get angry you may say things you later regret.

Fish

Seeing or catching fish suggests that you should be able to gain what you want if you look in the right places. Dead fish indicate quarrels and disappointment. *See also* Angling, individual fish.

Fisherman

Since fish represent things you need, a fisherman is someone who can provide those things for you.

Flag

A message or communication of some kind is likely to come to you telling you about a problem experienced by a friend or someone you know. If you act swiftly, you should be able to help them.

Flame

Flames tend to be considered a dream image representing slander, gossip, rumour or general bad feeling. Be aware that you may not be able to trust everyone around you. *See also* Bonfire, Fire.

Flattery

To be flattered in your dream usually suggests that you are uncomfortable about something in your life relating to your opinion of other people. Has something your partner's been doing been preying on your mind? Have you heard some gossip about a friend whom you trusted, but you don't know whether or not to believe it? There is no need to trust everything you hear. Make sure you have the full facts from the person concerned before you come to any rash judgements.

Flea

Fleas are a dream image suggesting minor annoyances or trivial issues that could be getting you down. You have the wherewithal to address the problems and make them go away.

Flirting

Flirting with someone in a dream generally suggests that you are preoccupied with one or more of your relationships and perhaps uncomfortable with the present situation. You may have been thinking about ending a relationship, or have some doubts as to whether you can entirely trust your partner. Honesty and good communication are usually the best things to rely on in such circumstances.

Floating

To see anything floating on water in your dream could be taken as a suggestion that you are taking things too easily and missing opportunities of improving your position. If you dream that you are floating on water, it suggests that you have the potential to do well for yourself and are in a good position to do so; if you are sinking, you are likely to be missing those opportunities.

Flood

Dreaming of being involved in a flood suggests something out of control in your life, which could potentially overwhelm you, although you have the means to deal with the problem if you apply yourself.

Floor

If you are scrubbing a floor that will not come clean, then you are worrying unnecessarily about minor problems. Try to find the cause and solve the problem; it is unlikely to be as troublesome as you think. Sitting or lying on the floor in a dream suggests that your next move should be upwards, so things are likely to improve in an area of your life.

Flower

Flowers are generally a positive image in a dream, indicating happiness, pleasure and consolation. If they are growing in profusion, your future is promising. Sweet-smelling flowers suggest pleasure and mutual affection, although if you pick them and they wither, it indicates that perhaps you should consider more carefully where you are placing your emotional trust. The warning is stronger if the flowers are red or dark in colour rather than white or yellow. Planting flowers suggests that you are creative and will work hard to cultivate what you want in life. *See also* Bouquet, Plant, individual flowers.

Flute

To play or hear someone playing on a flute or another wind instrument can suggest trouble and arguments. *See also* Music.

Fly

Being pestered by a swarm of flies suggests that you may have placed your trust in someone who did not deserve it, and you could encounter problems because of your decision. If the flies land on you, the problems are likely to more serious, although not insurmountable.

Flying

To dream of flying suggests that you are destined to succeed in life, and that your courage and perseverance will help you to overcome any obstacles you encounter. The best dream image is being able to fly and land at will. Flying backwards is not as positive an image, as it can suggest that you could be hampered by unwanted constraints. If you feel afraid as you are flying, then there is an issue of trust in your life that needs to be resolved. Have you misplaced your trust in someone, or have you contemplated going back on the trust you have offered to someone else? If you fall suddenly while you are flying, expect a disappointment. If you are surrounded by birds, you may have a wide range of new acquaintances. *See also* Wing.

Fog

To dream of being in a thick fog or mist is a dream image suggesting that you could be more in tune with the spiritual or metaphysical than the practical, or at a less fundamental level that you are in a state of confusion. Try to fix on a point of reference from which you can judge the best course of action.

Font

Seeing yourself at a baptism ceremony standing beside a font is a symbol of moving from one state to another. The precise interpretation depends on your circumstances. *See also* Baptism.

Fool

Deceit is suggested by dreaming of a fool, so you should be careful that no one tries to deceive you. If you are worried by the thought that you have committed a stupid act, then it could suggest minor problems, perhaps associated with overspending or with a rash decision.

Foot

The image of feet in a dream is traditionally thought to suggest the success of your relationships with others. To have extra feet or feeling that you are light on your feet is a good sign as it suggests you relate well with other people. If your feet are injured or sore, perhaps you could benefit from paying more attention to how you deal with people around you, particularly those closest to you. Your communication skills and your ability to understand other people's point of view could need attention. If someone or something is biting your feet, it suggests that someone is envious of you, while if they are scratching the soles of your feet, this is an indication of flattery. Washing your feet communicates the idea that you are trying to get rid of something or someone who is annoying you. To dream your feet smell bad signifies problems, especially related to communication with others and how they see you.

Football

Watching a game of football suggests that you may hear some unflattering or even slanderous rumours about someone you know, but are unable to say anything in their defence.

Forehead

Having a large forehead in a dream is a sign of ingenuity and sound judgement. If your forehead is made of metal, you are likely to be aggressive and intractable.

Forest

A dream in which you are wandering in a forest or wood predicts happiness, either personally or financially. If you are lost in a forest, however, it can indicate uncertainty in love. *See also* Bramble, Tree.

Forgery

If someone else has forged your signature in a dream, you can count this as a lucky omen of financial advantage. However, if you have forged a signature, then the reverse could be true.

Forget-me-not

Forget-me-nots suggest that other people think well of you or have you in mind. *See also* Flower.

Fortune

If you are extremely wealthy in your dream, you may find that you are short of money for some time, but in the end you should be comfortably off. If you manage to amass a fortune through your own efforts in the dream, you could suffer losses, although you are likely to be able to turn the situation around by hard and patient effort. Being given a fortune in a dream should warn you to be cautious, especially in your financial dealings. *See also* Money, Treasure.

Fortune telling

If you are having your fortune told in your dream, your favourite ambition could be blighted if you continue in the same way of behaving. To dream you are telling a friend's fortune indicates that you could have a serious disagreement.

Fountain

A fountain of clear, running water indicates health, recovery and improvement, although if the water is dirty or brackish, then things are unlikely to improve in the near future. *See also* Water.

Fox

A fox symbolises a wary adversary. You may meet someone whose motives are not quite as clear-cut as they maintain. Be careful that no one betrays a confidence or treats you in an underhand way.

Foxglove

Foxgloves are an omen of true friendship. *See also* Flower.

Fraud

If you have been defrauded of something in a dream, you may need to lean on the support and help of your friends or colleagues. If you have committed fraud against someone else, you are likely to do someone a good turn, and they are likely to be very appreciative.

Friend

Dreaming of your friends is an image of happiness.

Frog

Frogs symbolise flatterers and indiscreet gossips. *See also* Toad.

Fruit

Fresh fruit, especially in season, is a positive dream image, suggesting health and happiness. Rotten fruit has the opposite meaning. *See also* individual fruit.

Funeral

Attending the funeral of someone close to you suggests a connection or new opportunity that is likely to benefit you or a friend. *See also* Coffin, Death, Grave, Hearse, Mourning.

Furniture

Traditional interpretation is that happiness always follows a dream of furniture: perhaps you will find success at work, a new partner or a new home.

Gallows

To dream about seeing a gallows is a dream of contrary, suggesting a long and happy life with plenty of good luck.

Game

To play at any party games or to watch a child playing in a dream signifies prosperity, pleasure, health and concord among friends and relations. *See also* individual games.

Garden

To dream that you are walking in a garden of flowers and among trees indicates that you are likely to find a great deal of pleasure through communication. *See also* Plant.

Gardening

If you are working in a garden in your dream, it suggests a creative streak. *See also* Digging, Plant, Rake, Weed.

Garlic

To eat or smell garlic signifies a discovery of hidden secrets and domestic arguments.

Geranium

You are likely to find that you grow more attractive to others in the not too distant future, and could find that you have to learn how to judge whether people are attracted to you just because you look good, or whether it is because they actually like you and enjoy your company. Those decisions will be important ones. *See also* Flower.

Ghost

If you are not frightened by a ghost in a dream and it feels like a benevolent presence, the dream is suggesting news from abroad or from an unexpected source. This tends to be a good dream. If you are afraid, however, then it is possible that something unfortunate may be around the corner.

Giant

A giant is a very positive dream image, indicating increase in business or general prosperity.

Gift

Receiving a gift in a dream is an indication that something positive is likely to happen to you quite soon. You may actually receive something, or just be given some good advice or find a positive change in your circumstances. If you are giving anything away, however, especially if you feel it is of value to you in any way, it can denote loss or unfaithfulness.

Gin

To dream of drinking gin indicates a short life with many changes. *See also* Drink.

Glass

Glass in a dream usually symbolises something important that you have been taking for granted. Broken glass generally indicates that something fragile has been damaged or has gone out of your life. This could relate to friends, relationships, an opportunity or even something material.

Glasses

Do you feel you are seeing things clearly or are you aware that you may be misjudging a situation, or that someone may be misjudging you? Dreaming about glasses suggests that you may want to look at things from a different perspective.

Globe

To dream about a globe is a suggestion that you are likely to have connections with people in several different foreign countries.

Glove

Wearing gloves in a dream is thought to symbolise passing happiness. Being given a pair of gloves suggests you may have to make choices between partners or friends. *See also* Clothes.

Goat

Goats are generally thought to suggest that you will get on well in life, even though you may have to surmount some difficulties and work hard to achieve what you set out to do. It is particularly favourable when you see them clambering about a mountainside. *See also* Animal.

Goblet

To drink out of a goblet indicates that good times are coming and you are likely to be happy. It represents both a sense of achievement and having fun.

God

Joy, comfort, grace and the blessing of God are all suggested by dreaming that He responds to your prayers.

Gold

Gathering up piles of gold is thought to suggest that your present course of action should be profitable and that you should gain materially. However, if you feel suspicious or cannot hold on to your gold, it can suggest that you could be unable to enjoy many of the material things you acquire because of some other unhappiness in your life. *See also* Treasure.

Goldfish

Dreaming of goldfish is an image suggesting work or financial problems. *See also* Fish.

Golf

Would it be a good idea to pay more attention to leisure and recreation than spending all your time working? This is the suggestion of a dream in which you either watch or take part in a game of golf.

Gondola

To dream that you are travelling in a gondola signifies an easy existence and independence through another's exertions. *See also* Boat.

Goose

A goose is generally considered to be an emblem of sincerity, and in a dream suggests good news, meeting up with an old friend, or a happy conclusion. *See also* Bird.

Gooseberry

Gooseberries are generally thought to be an image of fun and light-hearted things in your life. It could therefore indicate children, a good social life or perhaps a fun-loving partner. However, there is also the suggestion that this lack of seriousness may not necessarily be advantageous to you: someone could play a joke on you that backfires, or someone close to you could feel they could have more fun elsewhere than in your company. *See also* Fruit.

Government

If you dream that you work for the government, the meaning is usually thought to suggest that you regard responsibility and hard work very highly, and perhaps that you may be likely to have to support several others through your diligence.

Grain

Watching grain being gathered suggests profit and advantage.

Grandchild

Seeing your grandchildren in a dream, whether or not you actually have any, suggests connection with youth. You may have a grandchild, meet some old friends and spend time reminiscing, visit a school, or do anything that gives you a link to your past.

Grape

Eating grapes in a dream signifies cheerfulness and profit. Treading grapes for wine suggests that you will get the better of someone with whom you disagree. *See also* Fruit.

Grass

Cutting the grass is an image suggesting deceit.

Grasshopper

Grasshoppers are said to signify gossip.

Grave

The image of a grave in a dream is usually thought to represent change, and moving on from one thing to the next. While it can therefore suggest the end of something, it can also offer hope of the beginning of something else that could be better. *See also* Burial, Coffin, Funeral.

Gravel

A level area of gravel is a sign that your route through life may not be as smooth as you would wish, or as it might at first appear. Although raked gravel looks level and even, it is not always easy to walk across it.

Greenfinch

This image in a dream warns you to stick to your work if you want to avoid making a loss. *See also* Bird.

Greenhouse

Dreaming of a greenhouse is suggestive of a rapid improvement in some area of your life.

Greyhound

Greyhounds are a symbol of positive action and progress. *See also* Dog.

Grindstone

The comfort and advantages that you gain are most likely to be from your own efforts and you cannot expect to be given much to help you along in life. If you are grinding corn, however, you should be able to do well. Grinding coffee is thought to suggest that you may have difficulties at home, while grinding pepper suggests some unhappiness in your life.

Guest

To dream that a large number of guests suddenly descend on you expecting hospitality suggests that you could lose contact with some close friends.

Guitar

Playing the guitar usually relates to success in relationships, especially if you are playing or listening to a beautiful melody. *See also* Music.

Gun

Hearing a gunshot in the distance suggests you are likely to receive some unexpected news. If you are handling or firing a gun, it indicates a long-standing quarrel and that you should be careful not to take any action that you will later come to regret. *See also* Cannon.

Gypsy

Dreaming of a gypsy suggests that you want to travel and are more than likely to fulfil those ambitions.

Hail

Dreaming that you are in a hailstorm is an image that suggests that you may have to put up with obstacles or behaviour from colleagues or friends motivated by envy. But if you persevere with what you know is the right path for you and are not distracted, you are likely to succeed.

Hair

Being concerned with your hair in a dream is about self-image and how you view yourself in relation to others. Beautiful, well-groomed hair in a dream is an image of friendship, joy and prosperity, showing that you are happy with yourself and how you communicate with others. Dirty or untidy hair therefore has more negative connotations, while to lose your hair indicates annoyance or loss of some kind. Plaited hair suggests annoyance or quarrels. *See also* Bald, Combing, Shaving.

Hairdresser

Again related to self-image, seeing yourself having your hair done in a dream suggests either that you want to make changes to your image, or perhaps that someone is trying to influence you in ways that you do not necessarily want.

Hammer

To dream of using a hammer indicates that you are most likely to be able to shape your life in the way you want it to go. *See also* Tool.

Hand

Hands in a dream are symbolic of your ability to earn a living and look after yourself. Therefore if your hands are larger and stronger than usual, or if you seem to have lots of hands, you can expect to be able to achieve good things at work and to look after your family or dependants. If your hands are injured, then difficulties in those areas may follow. If your hands are chapped or sore, you could experience problems with one of your children or a member of your close family.

Handcuffs

Handcuffs are an image of involvement and responsibility. You may need the help of others, or someone you know may need your support, although if you co-operate with others, you are likely to be successful.

Happiness

Exercise caution after dreaming of feeling excessively happy in a dream, as it could mean that you are on the edge of a very difficult situation. However, if you meet any difficulties head on, you should be able to resolve them.

Harbour

To see a harbour in a dream suggests good news.

Hare

If you see a hare running in your dream, it is considered to be a sign that you can achieve considerable wealth by applying your intelligence, but if you are chasing the hare and it escapes, you may not be so lucky. *See also* Animal.

Harp

Playing a harp in a dream is not considered to be a good image, but one indicating envy or nervous problems. It suggests the need to create harmony rather than the fact that harmony exists. *See also* Music.

Hat

Wearing a smart hat in a dream indicates happiness or success, although if it is battered or dirty, it can suggest a similarly damaged reputation. If the hat is extremely exotic and showy, you may be viewed as vain or overbearing. If your hat is blown away and you are chasing it, you may lose face or find your reputation damaged. *See also* Clothes.

Hazelnut

To see or eat hazelnuts in a dream can be an indication that you have some difficulties to face up to. *See also* Nut.

Head

To dream that your head is large generally indicates that you are most likely to be successful; if it is small, you are likely to lack self-esteem and energy. To dream that you have the head of a wild animal indicates that you can call on the strengths of that animal to help you. If you dream that you have three heads on one neck, it suggests domination, power and reputation.

Headache

If you dream of having a headache, you may be experiencing a crisis of conscience and feel unable make a difficult decision. Don't be tempted to do what you know is wrong.

Hearse

The symbol of a hearse in a dream suggests change; the end of one aspect of your life and, it is hoped, the beginning of another. *See also* Death, Funeral.

Heart

To dream that your heart is strong suggests long life, but if you dream you have a pain in the heart it can indicate problems of ill-health either for you or someone close to you, although they are not necessarily serious.

Heather

Heather suggests good luck and a pleasant journey, as long as it is not withered. *See also* Flower.

Hedge

A hedge is a symbol either of a protective framework or of barriers to what you want to achieve. Try to view obstacles as a challenge rather than being defeated by them.

Hedgehog

If you see a hedgehog in your dream, you should be careful to protect yourself from people who might want to take advantage of your good nature. *See also* Animal.

Herb

Searching for herbs in a dream is an indication that you are looking for a solution to a work-related problem. Finding, smelling or eating fragrant herbs suggests that you are a hard worker and not afraid to put yourself out to achieve what you desire. *See also* individual herbs.

Hermit

As a dream image, a hermit is a symbol of sorrow.

Hiding

To dream that you are hiding suggests that you expect some bad news that could dash your hopes.

Hill

Travelling over steep hills in a dream suggests that you may encounter many difficulties in your path through life. You may gain some indication of how you will succeed by the success of your journey in the dream. Sitting with someone on the brow of a hill indicates that you should think carefully and make sure you know them well before you decide to make them a companion in your life, as it could be that they will make an unsuitable partner.

Hole

To dream you creep into or fall into a hole suggests that you could come into contact with undesirable people. *See also* Falling, Precipice.

Holly

The sharp leaves of the holly bush indicate disagreements or anxiety. *See also* Tree.

Homosexuality

This dream suggests that you are trying to resolve a conflict, perhaps between different aspects of yourself or perhaps in an area to do with your relationships with others.

Honey

Honey is an image of pleasure, prosperity and renown, although if the honey is surrounded by bees, you may find that others are jealous of your success. It also has suggestions of fertility and sexual activity.

Horn

Having horns on your head in a dream suggests power, although you should be careful to use it wisely.

Horse

Seeing or riding a horse in a dream suggests sound finances and a generally happy life. If the horse does not belong to you, you may come into money through luck, marriage or an inheritance rather than through your own efforts. If the horse stops and refuses to move, look to make changes if you want to progress. If the horse runs away with you and you are out of control, perhaps you need to modify your ambitions for a time. If you hear a horse neighing but cannot see it, then you could need to look hard to find financial success and make the right choices if you are to succeed. *See also* Animal, Riding.

Horseshoe

This is a traditional symbol of good news and also of protection, unless the horseshoe is pointing downwards in which case the luck it represents could be running away. Because of its social significance, it is also related to news of weddings.

Hotel

To dream of living in a hotel signifies that you may shortly have to move, travel or live temporarily in new surroundings.

House

Having a dream in which you build a house suggests comfort, although seeing one knocked down indicates problems if you continue on the same course of action.

Hunger

If you dream of being extraordinarily hungry, you are likely to be ingenious and hard working. *See also* Eating, Famine.

Hurricane

If you dream of a hurricane, it can be an indication that you feel you are being drawn into a serious quarrel against your will or better judgement. You are feeling out of control. Stand your ground, otherwise you could feel that negative influences are too strong to resist and you may find yourself in a difficult situation. If the worst comes to the worst, radical change sweeping past you should give you opportunities to start again. *See also* Wind.

Hypnotism

To dream that you have been hypnotised indicates that if you are not careful you could reveal a confidence that could cause unpleasantness to some of your friends.

Ice

Dreaming of ice and snow out of season suggests hindrances to your plans. To dream you are sliding or skating on ice denotes that you could pursue an unprofitable concern and lose out.

Iceberg

Someone may take advantage of his or her superior position to harm you in some way.

Illness

If you dream that you are suffering from an illness, it suggests unhappiness or constraint, but if you are being well looked after, then you have little to worry about in the long term. Seeing yourself tending the sick suggests happiness. *See also* Invalid.

Indigestion

Something is disgreeing with you or you are feeling that you can no longer tolerate a particular situation. Action needs to be taken to resolve the issues that are worrying you, and perhaps you need to look for new ways to overcome those problems. It can sometimes be helpful to break down an issue into smaller, more manageable, sections and deal with one thing at a time.

Injection

Being given an injection can suggest that someone is invading your privacy or trying to force their opinions on you, but if you are giving the injection, the reverse might be true.

Injury

To dream you receive an injury warns you to beware of strong opposition, especially at work.

Insanity

If you are aware in your dream that you are behaving in an insane way, it is a very positive image of future success. *See also* Madhouse.

Insects

You are concerned about something that may appear insignificant but is causing you considerable annoyance if you dream about insects. If there are many of them, it may be that you are experiencing a sense of powerlessness in the face of circumstances. More aggressive insects, such as wasps, could also suggest danger.

Insult

To dream that you have been insulted is an image relating to inefficient communication. You may be involved in a business dispute, or someone may try to take advantage of you by flattering you when they are insincere.

Intestines

In dreams, your intestines traditionally symbolise your family and those closest to you. If you dream that you have been cut open but cannot see your entrails, you could experience a problem or loss related to your family. However, if you have been suffering from problems related to your family, this same image could indicate that those problems should be solved. To eat entrails means you could be in a position to gain in some way through a family connection.

Invalid

If you see yourself as an invalid in a dream, you may suffer a setback to your health but it is unlikely to be either serious or of long duration. Comforting or caring for an invalid in a dream suggests bad news concerning someone close to you. *See also* Illness.

Invisible

To seem to be invisible in a dream suggests that you are worried about the effect you are able to have on important decisions – or more precisely you are concerned that your input is not valued or regarded. Developing your own self-esteem and thinking through your own opinions should help you to communicate them more effectively.

Iron

The strength of iron is the crucial part of this dream image, suggesting problems, arguments or damage of some kind.

Island

An island is an image of isolation. You may feel the support of others is lacking, or you may be about to lose someone important from your life through travel or the diminution of a friendship.

Itch

Dreaming that you are itching suggests that you are worried by minor problems but you are likely to deal with them effectively.

Ivy

Perhaps because it can hold fast, ivy is an image of faithfulness, enduring relationships and the support of friends. *See also* Plant.

Jasmine

This sweet-smelling flower is an indication of good luck. *See also* Flower.

Jealousy

Dreaming about jealousy signifies trouble and anxiety.

Jewel

A single, rare jewel in a dream suggests that you should be less inclined to judge people harshly. Someone close to you could become a valuable friend if you make the effort to recognise his or her worth. However, if you are blinded by the jewel, make sure you are judging others honestly. If you seem to own many jewels, you could expect a gift or financial advantage of some kind, although if the jewels are green, envy or jealousy could be involved in the situation. *See also* individual jewels.

Journey

The journey has always been a symbol of life, so to dream of setting out on a journey, by whatever form of transport, suggests that you are about to experience a change in your circumstances, or undertake something new. Think about the experience of the dream journey to see more about whether that change is likely to be for the better and how it relates to what has gone before.

Judge

Dreaming of a judge suggests that trying to improve things you are not happy with could result in you making matters worse rather than better. Make sure you protect yourself from people who do not have your best interests at heart, and plan changes carefully before you act. *See also* Court case, Magistrate, Law, Lawyer.

Jug

To dream of drinking out of a jug is a sign that you may soon be embarking on a journey. If the jug is large, the journey could be long; if small, the journey could be short. Breaking a jug generally indicates a surprise or an unpleasant interruption.

Jumping

To dream that you are jumping from a high position or over obstacles is a sign that you are likely to meet with lasting success if only you put your heart and soul into your work. *See also* Leaping.

Jungle

If you dream of being lost in a jungle, be careful that you are not misled by someone close to you. If you meet a wild animal in the jungle, you could be pestered by this person for some time.

Jury

In a dream in which your attention is mostly given to the jury, you are likely to suffer a good deal of annoyance from the unreasonable conduct of one of your neighbours. If you dream that you have been summoned to serve on a jury, it is a sign that you could have trouble with your co-workers that could lead to a serious disagreement. *See also* Court case.

Kaleidoscope

An image of beauty and creativity that is nevertheless constrained and controlled by the kaleidoscope itself and so not given full rein. Perhaps you are feeling the need to break out and express yourself in new ways.

Keg

A keg is generally considered to be a sign of danger or hypocritical friends who are ridiculing you behind your back. Try to be as open and honest as you can and perhaps that will encourage others to do the same.

Kettle

A kettle is a symbol of happiness at home.

Key

To dream you lose your keys suggests that you are storing up anger about something. To dream you find a key denotes admission to a position of trust. If you are carrying a bunch of keys, look for new responsibilities in your life.

Keyhole

To dream that you see a person looking through the keyhole of your door is a sign that someone is trying to take something from you, but they are unlikely to be successful.

Kicking

Kicking something suggests the need to move something forward and is an expression of frustration, either with yourself or with others.

King

To dream you are talking with a king signifies a good reputation, and if he gives you something, that suggests gain and joy. *See also* Queen, Royalty.

Kiss

To dream of kissing your father or mother, or a member of your close family, suggests that you have good friends. If you kiss a deceased person, it signifies long life.

Kite

Dreaming of flying a kite indicates advancement at work and potential financial success, although if you are watching others flying kites, then you may well not benefit from that potential and should be more careful where your finances are concerned.

Knee

The knee denotes hard work and commitment, therefore if you dream that you have hurt your knee, it indicates that you could be prevented from working efficiently for some reason. This will not necessarily be physical but could suggest that someone could hamper your efforts at work, or that you may not have the right tools to do the job properly. If your knee heals, then things are likely to improve. Swollen and painful knees suggest work-related problems.

Kneeling

To dream you are kneeling signifies anxiety about your affairs.

Knife

To dream you give someone a knife signifies injustice, disagreements and deceit. If you receive a knife from someone, it may be that you will have to cut the connection with something that you have valued.

Knitting

If you dream you are knitting your undertaking is likely to be successful. Someone else knitting signifies that you could be deceived.

Knot

To dream of knots suggests that there may be many things in your life that have the potential to cause you anxiety. Perhaps you feel that you are being prevented from resolving an issue, or moving a project forward, because of an insurmountable obstacle. Reviewing situations can often help to highlight ways to overcome them.

Laboratory

To dream of a laboratory signifies danger and sickness.

Labourer

To dream of a labourer signifies that you are likely to find yourself in a position to improve your financial position.

Lace

A dream of lace signifies extravagance, a carelessness with money or lack of good financial organisation. Consider whether you can better organise your finances so that you do not run into problems.

Ladder

A ladder in a dream is an image of a journey or progress, so if you are climbing a ladder and reach the top, you are likely to travel or to achieve your ambitions. If you are descending the ladder, however, it could be sensible to re-examine your prospects and perhaps consider a change of course. *See also* Climbing, Tool.

Lake

To dream of a lake of clear water suggests that life should hold more joys than sorrows for you, but if the water is rough, it can mean difficult times ahead. *See also* Boat, Sailing, Sea, Ship, Water.

Lamb

Seeing a lamb in a dream can be taken in different ways depending on the circumstances. If it is frolicking happily with its ewe, then it is an image suggesting comfort and happiness, but a lamb alone and bleating for its ewe is more likely to indicate that you may have misplaced your trust in someone, or in a scheme that you thought would be beneficial. *See also* Animal.

Lamp

A shining lamp is a good sign as it indicates improvement, usually either in health or relationships. If the lamp is broken or switched off, it can indicate a period of sadness or ill health. *See also* Light.

Landscape

To dream of seeing a landscape stretching out in front of you indicates that you are likely to experience some good luck.

Lark

To dream of soaring larks tends to suggest that there is a potential for financial gain in some way. *See also* Bird.

Laughter

Laughter is a spontaneous expression of happiness and lightness of spirit. However, if people are laughing at you, that is not the same thing at all: it is a deliberate and unkind act that suggests you are anxious that something you have done may be ridiculed.

Laurel

Dreaming of seeing or smelling a laurel bush is traditionally a sign of fertility, perhaps literally – meaning you are likely to have children – or perhaps meaning that you will be creative and successful in some way. A dream about a laurel tree, as with most dreams about trees, is a positive image, suggesting pleasure. It also has connotations of success and profit. *See also* Tree.

Law

If you dream that you are called to practise at the bar as a lawyer or that you are involved in a trial or law suit, this suggests arguments or confrontation of some kind, not necessarily legal, from which you should emerge successful. *See also* Court case, Judge, Lawyer, Magistrate.

Lawyer

It is said that dreaming of a lawyer indicates bad news or a loss on the horizon. *See also* Court case, Judge, Law, Magistrate.

Lead

To dream about handling lead is suggestive of illness or heavy responsibilities.

Leaf

To dream that the ground is covered with green leaves or you see a tree covered in green leaves is a positive image suggesting that you are happy with your life and moving in the right direction. If the leaves are withered, however, the dream suggests loss of some kind, or unrequited love. *See also* Tree.

Leaping

A dream in which you see yourself leaping over walls or obstacles suggests that you are likely to have to surmount a number of hindrances or obstructions in life, although you are likely to succeed if you persevere. *See also* Jumping.

Learning

To learn a lesson of any kind in a dream indicates that it would be advantageous to try to get out of the rut into which you have fallen, either by learning a new skill or taking a different direction in life.

Leg

Legs are an image indicating forward progress. If your legs appear strong and healthy, that is a good dream. However, if they are injured or swollen, you could be thwarted and find difficulty moving ahead as you would wish.

Lemon

Perhaps because of their sharp taste, dreaming of lemons is said to suggest arguments or sharp words in your family or among your immediate friends. *See also* Fruit.

Leopard

Dreaming of a leopard has a similar significance to dreaming of a lion, although the positive influence is likely to be more subtle. *See also* Animal, Lion.

Letter

Writing letters in a dream is usually associated with good news or success. Receiving letters is an indication that you should be alert for a chance comment from someone that will clarify a decision you have been trying to make. *See also* Writing.

Libel

If you dream that you have libelled someone, you are likely to be even tempered and moderate in your opinions and behaviour. Dreaming that you libel someone else suggests that your character is, in fact, above suspicion.

Library

To dream of sitting in the library means that you have abilities which, rightly cultivated, could enable you to attain literary distinction.

Licence

If you dream of taking out a licence for something, or filling in an official form, it could be that you want to change your occupation.

Lie

To dream that you have told a serious lie is an indication of honesty. If you hear someone else tell a lie, you may receive good news concerning someone close to you.

Light

Seeing a light shining in a dream is a positive symbol of happiness in one or more areas of your life, although if the light is suddenly switched off or disappears, it could indicate an unexpected problem or being parted from a friend. A gradually increasing light suggests either an intellectual improvement or growing skill of some description. *See also* Lamp, Torch.

Lighthouse

A lighthouse is a symbol of warning but also its light can guide you to safety. There may be something about to happen that you feel could be dangerous in some way, but if you are aware of the problems and use the help you are offered, you should be able to find your way out of any difficult circumstances.

Lightning

Flashes of lightning in a dream can indicate a change of location, or perhaps envy or jealousy among those around you. *See also* Rain, Storm, Thunder.

Lily

To see, hold or smell lilies out of season symbolises that your hopes of obtaining something are likely to be frustrated. *See also* Flower.

Lily of the valley

Generally thought to be indicative of relationships, dreaming of lily of the valley suggests that your partner is likely to be loving and down-to-earth, but not particularly ambitious. *See also* Flower.

Linen

Linen clothes are generally thought to suggest that you will be fortunate. *See also* Clothes.

Lion

A lion is a symbol of authority. To ride on the back of a lion suggests that you will have the support of someone influential, while if you are afraid of the lion or confront it, you are likely to argue with someone in authority. To see the head of a lion, or dream you have the head of a lion, suggests that you will accomplish your ambitions and perhaps become very powerful. Dreaming of a lion cub indicates influential friends. *See also* Animal, Leopard.

Lip

To dream that you have beautiful lips is a sign that your friends and family are healthy, but if your lips appear dry and chapped, it suggests the opposite.

Lizard

Dreaming about a lizard suggests changes, especially changes in business, and perhaps brought about by influences beyond your control. *See also* Reptile.

Lock

Seeing a closed lock in a dream suggests that you may have problems to overcome, but if you undo the lock, you are likely to succeed in getting the better of them. *See also* Padlock.

Loss

To dream that you have lost something of value suggests that there is something you are trying to hold on to, not necessarily something physical. You may either need to work harder to find ways to keep what is important to you, or recognise that things change and you have to learn to let go and move on.

Love

To dream of true love signifies happiness and success in relationships, although if you dream that someone you dislike is in love with you, be careful to cultivate friendship and respond positively to friends, otherwise you may find that they are not there when you need them.

Luck

To dream that you have experienced a stroke of good luck is a sign that you are inclined to leave too much to chance and that you should rely more upon your own judgement.

Luxury

To dream of enjoying yourself in the lap of luxury suggests potential disappointment and the need for change.

Lynx

A lynx is a symbol of a powerful and perhaps vicious enemy and suggests that you should perhaps be more cautious. *See also* Animal.

Machinery

To dream that you are working or inspecting machinery is an indication that you will not always need to work hard to earn your living.

Madhouse

For a young person to dream that they become an inmate of a madhouse is an indication that they might shortly be offered a post of responsibility and trust, where they will be required to take on many new responsibilities. They will be well regarded for sound judgement and good conduct. *See also* Insanity.

Magazine

Dreaming of reading a magazine is a fairly lucky image suggesting that you are likely to extend your education in some way, perhaps by taking a new job or learning a new skill. *See also* Reading.

Magic

If you feel as though you are under a magic spell in a dream, it could be a warning to make sure that you are placing your trust carefully. Someone may be using an underhand means to control you. *See also* Conjurer.

Magistrate

Make sure you not only act correctly but are also seen to act correctly, otherwise your actions or your motives may be misinterpreted. *See also* Court case, Judge, Law, Lawyer.

Magpie

If you see several of these birds congregated together, beware of foolish gossip that could lead you into trouble. *See also* Bird.

Make-up

If you are putting on make-up in a dream, the indication is that either you, or someone close to you, is trying to put a brave face on a situation, or trying to make themselves look their best for you. It is up to you to decide whether their motives are entirely straightforward, or whether they are trying to give you a false impression. Learn where you can safely place your trust.

Map

A dream in which you are studying a map is suggestive of change and possible travel. If the map is of your own country, it is more likely to indicate that you could experience changes in your circumstances, or meet up with someone you have not seen for some time. If the map is of a foreign country, the implication is that a journey is likely.

Marble

To dream of marble in any shape or form denotes that you should be successful against those who do not have your best interests at heart.

Market

To dream of being at a market is related to buying and selling. Perhaps you are trying to dispose of something you no longer require. If the market is busy, then the likelihood of your succeeding is greater.

Marriage

Traditionally, a dream of marriage is a negative image, suggesting difficulties ahead. *See also* Elopement.

Marsh

To dream that you are in a bog or marshy piece of land and manage to get through it, despite sinking in, suggests that you should be successful in whatever you attempt.

Mask

A classic image of deception, be careful that those you consider your friends or colleagues are not trying to deceive you.

Maze

To dream you are in a maze signifies that you are either trying to unravel a mystery or that you are likely to have one to solve before very long.

Meal

To dream you are eating a good meal signifies poverty, or the opposite if there is nothing for you to eat. *See also* Eating.

Medicine

If you dream that you are taking medicines, it suggests that you will have to make some radical changes in your life if you don't want to put up with many things that are disagreeable. To dream that you have just qualified to practise medicine suggests you could have a high degree of skill in the technical or scientific fields.

Melon

A melon is a symbol of improvement in health, or recovery from illness. *See also* Fruit.

Mermaid

An image of a mermaid is related to the unusual, especially unusual or especially talented children.

Meteorite

Difficulties are said to affect someone who dreams about a meteorite landing on the Earth.

Midwife

Something that has been on the cards for some time is likely to be revealed if you dream of a midwife.

Milk

Milk is a life-giving and positive dream image, so you can expect success and contentment – unless, of course, you spill it.

Mine

If you dream of a gold mine, it could indicate that you might lend money on a hazardous speculation. Remember that although a higher risk gives you a greater chance of substantial gain, it also involves a greater chance of losing everything.

Minister

Dreaming of a minister of religion suggests calm and a resolution of conflicts and arguments.

Mirror

Personal appearances are important to people who dream of a mirror, perhaps too important. Be careful that vanity does not cause problems for you.

Mist

You are experiencing a sense of confusion. If you can try to focus on what is important, then other things may become clearer. *See also* Fog.

Mole

Since a mole spends much of its life digging underground, this dream can suggest hard work that will not necessarily come to anything. *See also* Animal.

Money

The image of money in a dream can have a variety of interpretations depending on the circumstances. If you dream that you have been given a large sum of money, it suggests success in an important area of your life, but if you find or have money that you know does not belong to you, it can indicate that you may lose money. If you see money that you want but you cannot touch, it suggests that you may be deceived by appearances. *See also* Bank, Coin, Fortune, Purse.

Monkey

Dreaming of a monkey is said to indicate a deceit. *See also* Animal.

Monster

Dreaming of a monster is thought to signify unrealistic hopes.

Moon

The moon is a feminine image and a dream of the moon therefore usually relates to women in general or to women in your life. It is usually a positive image, but if it is obscured, it can indicate ill health. *See also* Eclipse.

Moth

To dream of moths flying around a candle flame, especially if they fly into the flame, can suggest that you should be wary of a business scheme. On the surface it may appear potentially profitable, but if you look into it, it could be damaging. *See also* Butterfly.

Mother

Generally a reassuring image in a dream, this can indicate a new start in your life.

Mountain

Seeing high and craggy mountains in a dream suggests that you are formulating new ambitions and goals. Succeeding in climbing a mountain indicates that you will succeed in your ambitions, while the difficulty of the climb can be indicative of the problems you may have in achieving your desires. If you have help in the climb, you are likely to gain support in life. If you fail, or if you are falling down the mountainside, you could experience serious difficulties or failure. Perhaps the dream suggests you should review your plans. *See also* Climbing.

Mourning

Seeing yourself in mourning is an image of contrary, suggesting that you will pass through difficulties and start again. *See also* Funeral.

Mouse

A mouse in a dream is indicative of shyness or perhaps that you are confused about an issue that is important to you. *See also* Vermin.

Moving house

This dream tends to indicate upheaval in your life.

Murder

Murder in a dream is a sign of drastic change, and the implications relate to the circumstances of the dream. To dream you are killed denotes loss to the person who has killed you, whereas to dream that you kill someone suggests a loss to you.

Mushroom

To dream of gathering mushrooms indicates the likelihood of several small surprises.

Music

Hearing beautiful music in your dream, of whatever style you prefer, suggests good news and contentment with life. Discordant music is a sign of impending difficulties or ill health. *See also* Concert, Opera, Orchestra, Wind instrument, individual musical instruments.

Nail

To dream of knocking nails into a wall or some article you are making is a sign that you are most likely to have to rely on your own endeavours. *See also* Fingernail.

Nakedness

Nakedness in a dream usually denotes openness and honesty, especially if the body is beautiful. However, if the person is ugly or deformed, or if you feel ashamed at seeing the naked person or being naked yourself, it is more likely to suggest that your conscience is bothering you about some past action and it could be advisable to change your course of action. At heart, you know what is right and wrong.

Navel

The navel is a symbol of your parents, so if this image is prominent in your dream, it suggests that you should be thinking more about them and their welfare.

Neck

The neck signifies power, honour, wealth and inheritances. If you see yourself with a strong and large neck, although not deformed, you are likely to become well known and wealthy. A slender neck indicates the opposite. To suffer a crick in your neck and have to hold your head on one side suggests difficulties and perhaps a loss of respect or damage to your reputation.

Necklace

A dream in which you are wearing an expensive necklace can be taken as a suggestion that you may have more money than happiness in relationships. If you are given a necklace as a present, it also suggests that you should not suffer material or financial problems, but that you may not necessarily find wealth sufficient to make you happy. To dream of breaking a necklace signifies a loss of financial advantages.

Neighbour

A dream about your neighbours may indicate a need to be cautious in your actions. Try not to lose your temper. If someone plays a practical joke on you, or you think they are trying to tease you, you will only make the situation worse if you overreact. Retain your sense of humour at all costs and you will soon see the funny side.

Nest

To dream of seeing an empty nest suggests disappointment, although if the nest contains eggs or young it is a promising sign that things should go well for you. You may be successful at work, be happy with your partner, or contented with your family and friends. *See also* Bird.

Nettle

Being stung by nettles suggests that you will overcome disappointments or problems that could otherwise hold you back. *See also* Sting.

Newspaper

Reading a newspaper in a dream is related to communication. You could receive an important letter or telephone call, or learn something unexpected at a meeting, for example. As with the news printed in the paper, you cannot necessarily expect to be happy about what you hear, or to believe everything. *See also* Reading.

Nickname

Tact is called for if you are calling someone by his or her nickname in a dream, or they are calling you by such a name. Try to think a bit more about other people's feelings and don't just barge in regardless. They may cover up the fact that you have offended them, but if they are not able to tell you how they are feeling it may be that the offence rankles.

Night

Dreaming that night is approaching shows that you are concerned about the future. You should consider your options as this dream suggests that your present course of action might lead to anxiety and even sadness.

Nightingale

To dream of a nightingale indicates good news, a success at work or in relationships. *See also* Bird.

Noise

Hearing strange noises in a dream when you do not know what they are or what causes them indicates that your position could be influenced by unknown factors, or things outside your control.

Nose

If your nose is larger than usual in your dream, it suggests wealth and power, but to dream of losing your nose symbolises loss of those things. A long nose suggests a good sense of humour.

Novel

Reading a light or enjoyable novel in your dream suggests that you have the powers of attraction to become popular with the opposite sex, although if the novel is serious and boring you are not likely to find it as easy to gain partners. *See also* Reading.

Number

Numbers between one and 78 are supposed to be lucky, with 49 the luckiest number. Apart from 343, which is also lucky, higher numbers are considered uncertain.

Nurse

Dreaming about being a nurse underlines your caring qualities and suggests a long and happy life.

Nursery

Spending time in a children's nursery suggests that children are not likely to figure large in your life. You might have a tendency towards a serious approach to life, which could create problems for you that need not exist.

Nursing

To be nursing a stranger suggests you could experience a great deal of trouble by offending someone unintentionally. If the person is a friend, they are likely to intervene in your life at an unexpected moment.

Nut

The hardness of nuts can be an image that you may have to face some difficulties in your life, but if you crack and eat them successfully and they taste good, then you are likely to overcome any obstacles and find a way out of your difficulties.

Collecting nuts could be an indication that you may be storing up problems for yourself. Finding a store of nuts unexpectedly can have opposite meanings, depending on the circumstances. You could encounter unexpected difficulties, or perhaps discover something that, through hard work, will be of considerable benefit to you.

However, a nut tree is a positive image. The combination in a dream can be interpreted in different ways depending on the details of the dream. Benefits are to be had if you can overcome the difficulties or obstacles in your way. *See also* individual nuts.

Oak tree

An oak is among the most stately and imposing of trees, and is a dream image generally indicating security, long life and material success. By contrast, if the oak has been felled or damaged, it can indicate loss. *See also* Acorn, Tree.

Oar

If you dream of being in a boat and losing one or more of the oars it is a symbol of potential loss of the influence of someone who has been important in your life. *See also* Boat.

Oasis

An oasis is a protected place set apart from its surroundings. You may feel that you are in such a place, or perhaps be feeling the need to retreat to one.

Oats

To dream of either seeing, handling or eating oats or oatmeal is generally taken to mean that you are likely to be of an economical disposition, sensible and homely. An alternative interpretation is that you are feeling too sensible for your own good, and want to sow a few more 'wild oats'.

Obituary

Reading an obituary usually relates to hearing news, especially of a wedding or a new relationship.

Observatory

To dream that you visit an observatory to view the stars or for astronomical study is a sign that you tend to be fond of solitude and retirement, and are most likely to choose a way of life devoted to a study that requires close application.

Offence

To dream you have given offence, or that you have had cause for taking offence, indicates the development of a friendship into something much stronger.

Office

To dream of an office suggests you have a fairly well-defined role in an office and probably relate to a structure or hierarchy. This dream is related to those feelings and how you perceive yourself in that system. If you are turned out of your office, the dream suggests loss of responsibility, authority or even property.

Oil

Vanity and deception are indicated by dreaming that you rub scented oils on to your body.

Olive

Seeing or smelling olives in a dream is traditionally a productive symbol. It could mean a flourishing relationship, children, prosperity or success at work. If you are having to gather the olives yourself, the indication is that you may have to work hard to achieve your success. Eating sweet olives suggests prosperity; eating bitter olives can indicate that you may have to do something that is morally distasteful. Dreaming of an olive tree in fruit is an image of peace, delight, harmony, freedom, dignity and achieving your ambitions. *See also* Tree.

Onion

Quarrels and disagreements figure largely in the interpretation of dreams involving onions, perhaps as a result of a discovery of a previously unknown fact. *See also* Vegetable.

Opal

Good luck should follow a dream that features an opal, as this stone suggests happiness. *See also* Jewel.

Opera

Being at an opera suggests difficulties in relationships caused by flattery, or by one of you giving more attention to others than to your partner. If you discuss the issues and take action soon enough, then you could avoid unsettling and unpleasant arguments. *See also* Music.

Orange

Oranges are thought to be a negative dream image, suggesting jealousy, bad temper and discontent. *See also* Fruit.

Orchard

If you dream that you are walking through an orchard, you are surrounded by positive images of growth, fertility and happiness. You are likely to have a loving partner and a happy family. *See also* Tree.

Orchestra

To dream that you hear or see an orchestra playing relates to your ability to communicate with others and to work in a team to a given end. If the music is discordant, it indicates that you feel there are clashes with others that need to be resolved. *See also* Music.

Organ

Organ music generally gives an atmosphere of seriousness to a dream, and this indicates that perhaps you may have to deal with something sombre in your life, although you are likely to deal with it with honesty and a sensible approach. *See also* Music.

Ornament

Extravagance or financially difficulties are generally thought to be suggested by a dream in which you buy or surround yourself with a number of ornaments. Perhaps you should think about learning some financial restraint, or organising your money more efficiently.

Orphan

There is a possibility that you will gain some considerable advantage through a complete stranger.

Ostrich

If you see this bird in your dreams, it is a sign that you are inclined to be conceited. Unless you think less of yourself and more of others you could find that you lose out on the respect of those around you. Be more aware of what others are thinking and feeling and don't bury your head in the sand. *See also* Bird.

Otter

An otter is a lithe and graceful creature but very difficult to get hold of. In a dream, the image suggests that you may find something hard to understand. It is likely to involve people you have long thought to be your friends, although experience could show you that they have been making slighting remarks behind your back, or even acting as though they had never cared for you. *See also* Animal.

Owl

Nocturnal birds such as the owl are a bad omen in a dream and suggest that you are likely to have problems in an important area of your life. This could relate to something coming to light that changes your opinion of those close to you. *See also* Bird.

Oyster

Oysters are a very positive dream image, since they are able to create beauty out of something that is discarded. It suggests that you are likely to do well at your job, have a happy relationship with your partner, or healthy children. Whichever area of your life is currently the most important to you should, by your own hard work be successful.

Packing

To dream that you are packing luggage for a journey indicates that you are likely to prefer your home territory and are not likely to be much of a traveller.

Padlock

Although you will probably never be in real financial trouble, you are not likely to have many things of great value that you will need to protect. *See also* Lock.

Pain

Suffering pain in a dream is generally an indication of problems, and the part of the body in which you experience the pain can give you a clue as to what may happen in your life. Family problems relate to stomach pains. Pain in the navel relates to issues with your parents. Pain in the chest suggests problems with relationships.

Painting

Painting a picture in a dream suggests that you may make some mistakes in life but you will come to be well regarded in the end.

Palace

If you dream about living in a palace or grand ancestral home, it suggests that you may be about to experience a change of circumstances for the better.

Pancake

Pancakes are a positive dream image of a contented life with few problems either at home or at work. *See also* Eating.

Pansy

This flower is a symbol of modesty. You are unlikely to be a high-flyer but other people who are close to you recognise your worth and value your friendship. *See also* Flower.

Pantomime

Be careful of joking with one of your friends who does not share your sense of humour. Something you say could be misconstrued, perhaps deliberately, and lead to an argument or a degree of ill feeling.

Paper

Clean sheets of paper suggest that you have the potential to do what you want with your life. If you tear the paper, then take more care that your plans are well structured. Perhaps a little more thought should be given to seeing things from all points of view so that you do not overlook anything crucial.

Parachute

You have the means to gain the freedom you seek.

Paradise

If you dream of being in paradise, it suggests that you will run your life well and honestly and that you have the ability to be successful and happy in whatever you choose, as long as you maintain your principles.

Parcel

A dream in which you receive a parcel indicates the loss of a valued possession. If you are holding a parcel, the dream suggests that you will be in control of something of value or importance that could affect both your own and other people's well-being.

Parent

Parents in a dream are representative of responsibility and continuity, so the meaning of the dream will vary depending on the circumstances depicted and your own situation. It may suggest, for example, that you will behave responsibly in a given situation, that you have behaved irresponsibly and will reap the consequences, or that you will be called upon to do something, perhaps against your first instincts.

Parrot

Parrots in a dream relate to communication and reticence. You may have been broadcasting secrets that were meant to be kept to yourself, or someone else may have been gossiping about you, or may have betrayed a trust that you placed in them, or they in you. *See also* Bird.

Party

To dream you have received an invitation to a party is a sign that you should soon hear of some good news, or make new friends. *See also* Dinner party.

Path

To dream you are walking in a broad path suggests that you are likely to remain in good health.

Pawnbroker

If you dream that you have been forced to pay a visit to a pawnbroker, the inference is that although you may be successful at first, if you do not follow up your success by thoughtful and sensible action, you are likely to lose the advantages that you have gained.

Pea

To dream of eating peas suggests that you are likely to be successful at work. *See also* Vegetable.

Peach

To dream of fresh, ripe peaches in season symbolises health and happiness, although if you dream of damaged fruit, they are more likely to suggest hopes that are unlikely to be realised. *See also* Fruit.

Peacock

A positive dream symbol, a peacock suggests that you are likely to do well in your chosen profession, and be happy with your partner. Either you or they may be more attractive or physically fit than academic, but that will support rather than detract from your happiness. *See also* Bird.

Pear

Delicious, juicy pears signify joy or pleasure: sour or bruised pears, the opposite. You may be presented with an opportunity to improve yourself and you should seize that opportunity or risk regretting that you could have made more of your life. *See also* Fruit.

Pen

Dreaming of a pen is considered to relate to difficulties in communication in relationships. Perhaps you are having difficulty telling someone how you feel about him or her, or perhaps you are separated from a lover.

Perfume

Dreaming of smothering yourself in perfume can indicate that you have too high an opinion of yourself.

Pheasant

Pheasants in a dream are considered to be symbols of good luck. *See also* Bird.

Photograph

Photographs are images of the past, so this image in a dream suggests that we are looking over past events, or perhaps past or even present relationships. Look at your own position, in particular in relation to those people appearing in the photograph. Do you want to review your attitude to them, or theirs to you? Try to be particularly attentive to the needs of others and try to resolve any arguments, but don't forget that your own needs are equally important.

Piano

A dream in which you are playing a piano is a favourable symbol suggesting that you may discover something of value where you least expect it. It can be related to your creativity. *See also* Music.

Picnic

The dream image of a picnic is indicative of fun and new relationships.

Picture

Seeing yourself admiring beautiful pictures in your dream indicates that you could be attracted into an unprofitable concern by misunderstanding what is involved, or even be the dupe of someone trying to mislead you deliberately. You may waste your time on a project that will never come to fruition. Think and examine anything carefully before you make your decisions so that you are sure you have thought through all the possible options.

Pig

The traditional interpretation of pigs in a dream is that they represent idle people, selfishness and greed. To dream of a litter of piglets suggests fertility. *See also* Animal.

Pigeon

Pigeons in a dream are considered a sign that you will have a happy home and be generally successful in life. Flying pigeons are often thought to indicate good news, especially from abroad. Hearing pigeons cooing denotes happiness. *See also* Bird.

Pine tree

To dream you see a pine tree signifies slow change or even laziness. *See also* Tree.

Plant

To dream of watching plants growing in a garden is a suggestion that you have been thinking about making a move – perhaps of location, perhaps of job – and that it could be the best thing for you. *See also* Fern, Flower, Garden, Gardening, Ivy.

Play

See Game.

Playing card

To play cards in a dream is suggestive of deceit; you should be careful that other people are not trying to undermine your efforts. It is also said to relate to your relationships, and that you should be careful to be honest with others and not trifle with their feelings.

Pocket

When you have something in your pocket, it is not visible to others but may be very important to you. Is there a vital issue that you are keeping from someone, or lack the courage to share with them?

Poetry

If you imagine that you are writing poetry, you could be too idealistic, especially with regard to your relationships, and would do well to try to think more about what actually is, rather than an ideal vision of how you would like things to be.

Poison

Are you aware that you could have to deal with something that you know you will not like, or will not benefit you? It is probable that such a difficult situation will prove unavoidable.

Police

To be in police custody suggests that you are concerned that you may be blamed for something that was not your fault. There may be steps you can take to resolve any miscommunication or confusion.

Pond

A clear pond, especially if fish are swimming in it, is a good dream image as it indicates good relationships. *See also* Water.

Porcupine

A porcupine is a symbol of problems at work. Perhaps there are some thorny issues that you are not sure how to resolve. Cautiously is probably the best way to proceed. *See also* Animal.

Postman/woman

Dreaming of a postman or woman suggests that you are looking outside yourself for the solution to a problem but it may be more likely to come if you look to your own skills and qualities.

Post Office

If you want to keep your secrets to yourself, a dream of being in a Post Office suggests you should be careful whom you bring into your confidence.

Potato

Planting potatoes in a dream suggests that you may be neglecting your opportunities and that if only you cultivated your ability, you would be much more successful. *See also* Vegetable.

Prayer

To dream you are praying devoutly suggests that you have confidence in some higher power than yourself and that it will bring you joy, comfort and happiness.

Precipice

To fall over a precipice in a dream is a warning that something is precarious in your life. Perhaps you are being too careless and risking an accident. Perhaps you have become involved with some people who have lower moral standards than you have and could tempt you into bad behaviour. *See also* Falling.

Pregnancy

A dream of pregnancy suggests that something is in the planning or development stages that will take some time to come to fruition.

Prison

Being in prison in a dream is suggestive of constraint, or having to do something against your will. You may feel confined and that you want to broaden your horizons but don't appear to be able to do so. It does not necessarily mean that you will not succeed in your ambitions, but you may have to fight against obstacles, or even do something that is against your better judgement.

Procession

To dream that you are watching a procession or parade suggests a degree of orderliness in your life that you find comforting.

Prostitute

You feel a need for an aspect of personality that you may not naturally possess; perhaps you want to break out and act wildly for a change. Are you usually too sensible all the time?

Public house

Enjoying yourself in a pub with friends is a comfortable image of contentment. You are likely to be happy with your social circle and your way of life. *See also* Drink.

Pudding

If you dream about eating a rich pudding, it suggests that perhaps you have been overindulging and should be more careful of your diet. *See also* Eating.

Puppet

A puppet of any kind has no control over its own actions, so if you are working a puppet in a dream, then perhaps you feel you are doing the manipulating, whereas if you see yourself as a puppet, then it could be time to take more control over your own actions.

Purple

Purple denotes happiness, prosperity and the respect of those close to you. *See also* Blue.

Purse

Finding a purse in a dream is a positive image as it suggests good things are likely to come your way. Losing a purse, however, indicates the likelihood of loss, perhaps of property or perhaps of a friendship. *See also* Money.

Puzzle

Working out a puzzle in a dream is a sign that you may have some difficulties to overcome that will tax your intellect.

Pyramid

Spiritual power is focused within the pyramid, which is a powerful symbol of the combination of mind, body and spirit.

Quarrel

Quarrelling in a dream is a general indication of upheaval or change. *See also* Argument, Discussion.

Quarry

To dream that you have fallen down a quarry is a striking image of potential difficulties to come for either yourself or your family or close friends.

Queen

To dream you see a queen signifies honour, joy and prosperity. *See also* King, Royalty.

Quicksand

A powerful image of insecurity and lack of control, dreaming of walking on quicksand suggests that you are anxious that events are moving ahead and you have no power to change them. Review your options and see if you can establish a means of restoring control.

Racing

To dream you are running a race is a good token suggesting success or good news. If you have to fight particularly hard to win, your successes are likely to be accompanied by a similar level of hard work and determination.

Radio

A clear image of communication issues dominating your mind, the radio may speak with authority – suggesting that you could benefit from sound advice from someone you respect – or be unclear and keep fading off the station – giving the impression that the advice you have been receiving is not as useful as you may have thought.

Railway ticket

If you dream that you have bought a railway ticket, this suggests an arrival, perhaps of an unwelcome visitor. If you have lost a railway ticket, however, the suggestion is of an enjoyable or profitable journey. *See also* Train.

Rain

Being pelted by heavy rain or a storm suggests problems ahead, although if the rain does not cause any damage you should be able to overcome them. Gentle showers are suggestive of success over any minor obstacles, particularly if the sun is shining. *See also* Storm.

Rainbow

A rainbow is a traditional image of promise, especially that things will improve. It can therefore be taken to be a general amelioration of your circumstances, good news or new opportunities.

Rake

Using a rake in the garden suggests that you will use the intelligence and skills you have for the benefit of others, possibly in an important or influential role.

Raspberry

Dreaming of raspberries indicates good news. *See also* Fruit.

Rat

Rats in a dream suggest that some people around you might think they know what you want better than you do, but if you exercise courtesy, good humour and common sense you will soon enlighten them. *See also* Vermin.

Raven

Ravens in a dream are an indication of mischief or sadness, especially if they croak. *See also* Bird, Crow, Rook.

Razor

If a razor features in your dream, be cautious about interfering in any confrontations or you may find you offend everyone. *See also* Shaving.

Reading

Dreaming you are reading is generally a positive image, indicating wisdom, learning or happiness, depending on what you are reading. It suggests that you are trying to expand your horizons and extend your useful knowledge. *See also* Book, Magazine, Newspaper, Novel.

Reflection

Are you too concerned with your own self-image to deal effectively with other people? Or perhaps you want to review how you see yourself and make some changes on that score.

Reptile

A reptile is an image of disagreements or quarrels, especially if you feel you have reacted, or are likely to react, instinctively to an adverse situation. If you are bitten in your dream, you could come off second best. You could have a subtle and powerful adversary. *See also* Lizard.

Rhubarb

To dream of rhubarb, either growing in the garden or cooked on the table, is a bitter-sweet image suggesting that something you want very much may not be within your grasp or, if you do achieve it, it may turn out differently from how you had anticipated. *See also* Fruit.

Rib

Ribs in a dream relate to close relationships, so if they are broken the dream suggests arguments or rifts with someone close to you.

Ribbon

Be cautious after a dream of ribbons. You may be tempted into an extravagance that you cannot really afford.

Rice

Rice in a dream usually indicates wealth or fertility. It can also relate to spiritual sustenance.

Riding

Riding a horse suggests control over someone or something, especially if it is a wild horse that has never been ridden and you manage to tame the animal to the saddle. This can give good or bad indications depending on your circumstances. For example, the dream could suggest that you will be well regarded at work and be in good control of your department or your company, or it could give the indication that you are too dominant in your relationships for them to be successful in the long term. To be thrown from the saddle when riding a horse generally suggests that your opinion of yourself is likely to take a knock. *See also* Horse.

Ring

To have rings on your fingers in a dream suggests love and respect. Losing a ring or having them taken or dropping from your fingers suggests loss, perhaps of a relationship or, in any event, of something you value. Receiving a ring as a gift indicates unexpected news relating to a friend or close family.

Rival

To dream that you have discovered a rival for the affections of your partner is one of the best omens in love affairs, suggesting that your relationship will be a happy and long-lasting one.

River

A flowing river with smooth and clear water indicates happiness and success in life, a contented family and a good job. If the river is rough, however, then you could encounter difficulties on your path. Swimming in a river signifies struggles ahead. Trying to cross a river and finding it difficult suggests you will experience frustration and delay in something that is important to you. *See also* Water.

Road

A broad, straight and even road stretching before you is lucky, whereas a narrow and twisting road along which you cannot see very far is not good. You are likely to have to make decisions without being fully conversant with the facts. *See also* Street.

Robbery

To dream that you are attacked and robbed suggests loss, either of something or perhaps someone you value.

Robin

To see a robin denotes that you will make many friends, although your character and temper are such that you are not likely to form a lasting relationship with anyone. *See also* Bird.

Rocket

A rocket can either represent male sexual power, or power in a more general sense.

Rocking

A comfort activity, rocking suggests that you need to get in touch with what really matters to you, and perhaps find some support or encouragement from others, rather than having to take all the responsibility all the time.

Roof

If the roof of a house is destroyed by fire in a dream, this indicates potential problems with the things that give you protection, perhaps your parents, your partner, your money or your job. *See also* Fire.

Rook

To dream you see a rook signifies a successful conclusion of business. *See also* Bird, Crow, Raven.

Room

To dream that you are in a strange room signifies that you can cope with changes of circumstances and may have to do so in order to accomplish your ambitions.

Root

Eating roots in a dream suggests deep-seated disagreements.

Rope

Rope is an image suggesting responsibility. This could mean the welcome responsibility of family and children, or it could suggest constraints – perhaps at work – that are holding you back. Look at what is important to you in your life and discard things that are giving you frustration and anger.

Rose

Roses are an image of happiness, love and success. *See also* Flower.

Rosemary

Rosemary is a traditional image of remembrance, so seeing or smelling rosemary in a dream could indicate that a forthcoming event will be memorable, or that you may have cause to think back to events of the past. *See also* Herb.

Rowing

To dream that you are rowing a boat on a river, where the water is calm and clear, gives promise that your dearest wish will be fulfilled. *See also* Boat, River, Sailing.

Royalty

A dream involving royalty, whether you see yourself as royal, or see a king or emperor, signifies that you will receive an honour, or gain in some other way. *See also* King, Queen.

Ruin

Whether it is through thoughtlessness or as a result of a positive decision, something in your life may have been abandoned. Are you sure you have not lost something valuable because of that?

Running

Running in a dream usually suggests that you are ambitious to get ahead, to accomplish things in your life. If you want to run but find you are prevented, your ambitions may be hard to realise and demand a great deal of hard work and determination on your part. Running from a relentless pursuer suggests that you will need to have all your wits about you to withstand some temptation that will be put in your way. If you feel that you are running in pursuit of something or somebody, this indicates that you are too fond of relying on your own judgement without taking other people's opinions or feelings into account. Unless you listen to the advice of your friends when it is offered, you could end up regretting your obstinacy.

Rust

Seeing an object covered in rust, especially if it was once beautiful, suggests that something you have been working for and looking forward to may not turn out quite as you expected. Perhaps your attitude is backward-looking, or possibly you need to 'spring clean' your focus in order to be able to move ahead.

Sack

Bundles of sacks in a dream suggest that an unexpected event could cause you to feel very uneasy.

Sage

To dream of this strong-smelling herb signifies hard work, trouble, sadness and weakness. *See also* Herb.

Sailing

Sailing on calm water denotes a peaceful life, but if the weather is bad and the water rough, it can indicate problems.

Sailor

Talking to a sailor in a dream suggests news from abroad.

Salmon

Whether you are fishing for salmon or eating it, the suggestion of this dream image is that you are likely to see much of the world before finally settling down. *See also* Angling, Fish.

Salt

Salt is suggestive of the apparently small things in our lives that nevertheless have major impact in bringing variety and satisfaction. Do you feel that you life is lacking 'spice'?

Saucepan

An omen of difficulties, perhaps several problems 'coming to the boil' at once and needing attention. It could be that you are trying to cope with too many things all at once.

Sausage

Sausages in a dream are generally thought to indicate domestic problems.

Sawing

Sawing wood is an image that symbolises mistakes, doing something you regret or breaking off friendships or alliances that you later realise were important to you and should have been cherished rather than discarded. Think more carefully before you get into an argument with someone close to you. If you offend them thoughtlessly the consequences could be worse than you realised. *See also* Tool, Wood.

Scab

Seeing yourself covered with scabs symbolises anxiety and issues that annoy you and won't go away. Try to find an objective view of your circumstances, or of issues that you have to deal with. If you can define the problem, the solution may become clearer to you.

School

An image of a school suggests that an opportunity may soon present itself to you, either to improve your education or to widen your knowledge generally, or in some way to help you to advance yourself. Watch out for such an opportunity and do not let it pass you by, or you will regret the decision for a long time.

Scissors

Using scissors to cut something can be taken as a warning that if you divide your attention between two goals you are in danger of not realising either of them. Concentrate rather than divert your energies.

Screaming

Hearing screaming in a dream is an indication that you should be attentive to the needs of your friends as they may require your help before long. If you are screaming, you may hear something that will benefit you.

Screw

The image of a screw in a dream suggests that perseverance is likely to be the key to success. *See also* Tool.

Sea

Water in a dream is often considered to be a symbol of the path of your life. If the sea in your dream is blue and moving gently, you can expect a good time ahead of you. If it is completely calm, then you may experience delays or need to put additional energy into moving forward. A stormy sea obviously suggests a difficult time ahead. If you fall into the water, you may be overwhelmed by difficulties for a time. *See also* Drowning, Sailing, Shipwreck, Water.

Searchlight

In order to progress, look for focus in your decision-making and take guidance when it is offered.

Seashore

Sitting or walking by the seashore in a dream is a symbol of change, movement or travel.

Sex

Dreaming about sex can have very specific interpretations depending on personal circumstances, so you need to consider the symbolism in the dream and how that could relate to your own circumstances. It often relates to the need to feel closer to other people and to communicate better with them, or perhaps that you are looking for a closer, more physical relationship with someone. If the sexual act involves some fetish, it can suggest an immature outlook or a fear of sex; it could also suggest that you are trying to avoid opening up to someone. If sex is interrupted, it can indicate that something is holding you back. Having sex fully clothed in a dream often indicates guilt. Homosexuality in a dream suggests that you are looking for someone similar to yourself, not necessarily on a physical level. *See also* Homosexuality, Kiss, Love.

Sewing

Seeing yourself sewing in a dream is a symbol of creativity and hard work. You are likely to be well liked and happy in the possession of a close family and good and trusted friends. If you prick yourself with the needle while sewing, however, minor annoyances or anxieties are likely. *See also* Embroidery.

Shadow

A prevalence of shadows in a dream suggests that you may be ashamed of something you have done. You have it in your power to rectify your past mistakes.

Shaving

Being shaved in a dream, especially if your whole head is shaved, usually has negative connotations, indicating exposure or disappointment. However, if you have nothing to hide, you may choose to take things into your own hands and tell people something you have been hiding from them. *See also* Bald, Hair, Razor.

Sheep

Sheep in a dream are generally considered to be a sign of good luck, especially at work or in relationships, and the more sheep there are, the better the indications. *See also* Animal.

Shell

A shell is a hard exterior that protects a soft creature, and is a clear image of your anxiety that you are vulnerable, especially to emotional attack. Only by feeling stronger in yourself can you overcome that feeling of insecurity. Focus on your strengths and not your weaknesses.

Ship

Water in a dream is usually indicative of your path through life, so if your ship is moving well, you should encounter few problems, although if the water is rough, then you may encounter some difficulties. *See also* Boat, Drowning, Sailing, Sea, Water.

Shipwreck

A shipwreck not only suggests difficulties in life but can also suggest that your friends or colleagues are not being as honest and straightforward with you as they might.

Shirt

Dreaming of putting on a shirt is thought to suggest that you will generally enjoy a good life without serious mishap. *See also* Clothes.

Shoe

Being strongly aware of an image of shoes in a dream relates to reputation and standing in life. A smart pair of shoes suggests that you are down-to-earth and know where you are going. Being without shoes, or wearing old and tatty shoes, suggests problems. Wearing new shoes can indicate a new and prosperous direction in life. *See also* Barefoot, Clothes.

Shooting star

A shooting star in a dream is a sign of passionate love or high emotion.

Shopping

To dream that you are shopping suggests a concern that either your spending habits or your lifestyle are overindulgent and you should perhaps be more cautious in your approach to life, or exercise more economy with regard to money. *See also* Spending.

Sight

To dream that you have clear sight is an excellent omen of good health, although weak sight suggests possible ill health or a period of inactivity or confusion. *See also* Blindness, Eye.

Signpost

A signpost in a dream is an image of change of direction and the need for honest and straightforward dealing.

Silk

Wearing silk suggests prosperity, as does sewing silk. Trading in silk is a symbol that you are confident of success in business. *See also* Clothes.

Silver

Collecting up silver, especially if you are trying to hide it, suggests deceit, perhaps on your part or on the part of a so-called friend or colleague. Make sure that you are really able to trust those you live and work with. Eating silver suggests that you could be storing up anger.

Singing

Singing in a dream is a sign of consolation, so may suggest that you are likely to experience a problem that will require help and support, or that you are already on the right road and things are improving. *See also* Music.

Skeleton

If you see a skeleton in a dream it is a sign of anxiety about the crucial issues of something, possibly related to your home life. *See also* Bone.

Skin

To dream that your skin has become pale or yellow suggests poor health, while to believe in a dream that your skin is damaged or sore suggests deceit.

Sky

A clear and beautiful sky is a symbol that you are confident that you are well regarded by others. A cloudy sky, however, is suggestive of a less easy time in your relationships with those around you. *See also* Cloud.

Sleep

See Asleep, Tiredness.

Slipper

A symbol of the comforts of home, being conscious of the image of slippers in a dream suggests that your attitude should ensure that forthcoming relationships are successful. *See also* Clothes.

Smoke

To dream of seeing smoke, especially if you cannot see any fire, suggests that early successes may be short lived if you cannot overcome the difficulties you appear to be anxious about. *See also* Fire.

Smoking

To dream of smoking indicates waste and missed opportunities. Are you making the most of the circumstances in which you find yourself?

Snail

Snails are an image of inconstancy and change. *See also* Animal.

Snake

Traditionally, the image of a snake in a dream suggests envy, trickery or dishonesty, because of its association with the Garden of Eden. This is especially true if the snake bites you. If you fight with snakes and kill them, this is an indication that you will overcome such problems. The snake can also be seen as a powerful sexual symbol that you are trying to come to terms with your own sexuality. *See also* Animal.

Snow

To dream of snow in summer denotes that what you have will be protected. However, if the snow is melting away, then you need to be careful that you do not lose what you have worked hard to achieve.

Soldier

Soldiers are a sign of conflict, and the circumstances in the dream may give an indication as to how conflict is likely to come into your life and how it may be resolved.

Soup

Dreaming of eating or making soup is a comforting and homely image suggesting good luck. *See also* Eating.

Sparrow

To dream of sparrows denotes that you are likely to have to succeed through your own enthusiasm and hard work. You may not be hugely successful or well known, but you will have enough to live comfortably with your family. *See also* Bird.

Spear

A strongly masculine image with phallic connotations, this dream suggests that you feel powerful and able to confront issues head-on.

Speechless

Seeing someone in a dream who cannot speak is a symbol of mildness and gentleness. If you dream that you are married or closely connected with someone who does not speak, it is an image suggesting that they will be known for their communication skills or volubility.

Spending

To dream that you are spending extravagantly is a sign that you should be successful in your household management as long as you do not give in to too much extravagance. *See also* Shopping.

Spider

Perseverance is the message if you see a spider or spiders in your dream. It may be that you have been discouraged by recent events, but if you stick to your principles and continue to work hard and not give up, then success is likely to be yours in the end. If the spiders are crawling over you, then you are likely to be fortunate, perhaps even come into money from an unexpected source. Watching a spider spinning a web is also an indication of improved finances.

Spinning

To dream of spinning indicates that you see yourself as diligent and industrious and are generally happy with your outlook on life as it is proving creative and successful.

Splinter

Something could be irritating you. If it is sufficiently important, you would do well to deal with it and move on.

Squirrel

Squirrels are an image of bad temper or cunning. You may become involved with someone who proves to have a fierce temper, or be responsible for showing ill temper yourself. Another possible interpretation is that someone will try to defraud you, pick an argument, or otherwise undermine your position at work. *See also* Vermin.

Stag

The dream image of a stag is indicative of profitable investment and business success, although if you are chasing a stag and injure it or fail to catch it, this can suggest your concern that you will not be successful. Make sure you are confident of your ground before you proceed; ask for more information if that is what you need to make the decision. *See also* Animal, Deer.

Star

To dream you see a clear starry sky signifies prosperity and advantage, especially if you are involved in a voyage or journey. It can mean that you can expect good news from which you are likely to profit. However, if the stars fade, then you can anticipate that things may not go as well for you as first indications suggest. If the stars fall on top of you, this is an indication of problems.

Starling

To dream you see a starling suggest something minor is irritating you. *See also* Bird.

Sting

If you have been stung by an insect, the implication is that you could be about to enter a period beset by minor but annoying difficulties. *See also* Bee, Nettle, Wasp.

Stomach

If your stomach has grown larger and fatter than usual, this suggests material advantage to you and your family. You could receive a gift or a pay rise, or benefit in some other way. If your stomach is large but empty, you may not have material things, but you should maintain a good reputation and be well regarded by those around you. If your stomach is thin and shrunken, you could avoid a bad accident. A stomach-ache is indicative of family problems.

Stone

To dream of having a stone thrown at you denotes that you should think about being more tactful in your dealings with others. You can't expect friends or colleagues to be pleased with you if you criticise them too bluntly. Aim for a little more subtlety in your approach.

Stork

A pair of storks is a traditional dream image of marriage and fertility, but flocks of storks in a dream suggest the coming either of bad weather or perhaps bad company. *See also* Bird.

Storm

Dreaming of a storm tends to indicate pent-up anger or potential problems. If you release your anger in a controlled way, then you are more likely to be able to move to a period of calm. *See also* Lightning, Rain, Thunder.

Stranger

The return of a long-lost friend, or the renewal of some aspect of your life from the past, is indicated by a dream in which you meet, and especially talk to, a complete stranger. If you exchange something with them, it is a positive symbol for work-related aspects of your life. If you fight with them, you can expect to win arguments or gain promotion.

Strawberry

A positive dream image, strawberries represent fertility, love and a good-tempered family. *See also* Fruit.

Street

Dreaming of a city street often indicates that you are considering a move away from a busy or urban environment and that the move is likely to be beneficial. *See also* Road.

Stumbling

Watch your step, metaphorically, at work as you could be in danger of suffering in some way through an accident or innocent misfortune.

Sun

The sun represents unity, truth, light, abundance and wealth, so there could not be a more positive dream symbol. It can suggest the resolution of problems, happy relationships with family and friends, and good times at work. If the sun is clouded or obscured, however, then this represents a diminution of your prospects and perhaps that you will not find things as easy to achieve. *See also* Sunrise, Sunset.

Sunrise

Sunrise is an image of new beginnings, with the release of positive potential. It is up to you to realise that potential. *See also* Sun, Sunset.

Sunset

This may be an image of closure and ending, but the conclusion of one episode of your life can only mean the beginning of a new one, so it is not necessarily a negative dream. It is up to you how you view and cope with the changes that are likely to occur in your life. Try to avoid looking back and regretting what has been; instead look forward and see new options as challenges not problems. *See also* Sun, Sunrise.

Swallow

Good news and a happy home life are suggested by dreaming of a swallow or swallows. It is also sometimes said to suggest a journey. *See also* Bird.

Swan

A swan is a positive symbol in a dream, indicating a happy marriage, good relationships and good health. In particular, it represents constancy in relationships. *See also* Bird.

Sweeping

Care and attention to the important things in life are indicated by a dream in which you see yourself sweeping. You are likely to enjoy the company of your family and be happy to spend a good proportion of your time working for them and ensuring that they have everything they need.

Sweet

Eating sweets in a dream is traditionally thought to indicate subtlety. Could you require more subtlety in your dealings with others, or is it more likely that they need to be more tactful and observant in their dealings with you?

Swimming

Hard work and determination are the usual interpretations of seeing yourself swimming in a dream. If you manage to keep your head above the water and are getting along well, then this is a good sign that you will achieve your ambitions, in whatever direction they may lie. If you are swept along in a swift current, however, or find difficulty in swimming, then you could experience difficulties or disappointments. *See also* Water.

Table

A dream in which a table is the most prominent object suggests that your life is likely to be calm and methodical, without any startling events to disturb the equanimity.

Tablecloth

A dirty tablecloth in a dream suggests that you will always have plenty of the material things in life and are never likely to go short.

Taffeta

The fabric taffeta symbolises wealth without satisfaction. Although you are likely to achieve your worldly ambitions, they may not necessarily bring you happiness. Try to strike a balance. Remember that you can't always buy the things that will make you happy. *See also* Clothes.

Tamarind

To dream of tamarinds generally has negative connotations, perhaps because it is an exotic image for a Western dream. There could be bad news from abroad, or failures or problems of some kind. *See also* Fruit.

Taming

To dream you tame wild beasts suggests that you will have damaging problems to overcome. *See also* Animal.

Tea

Your many joys in life are likely to be interspersed with sorrow if you dream of drinking tea. Take care not to overlook the good times; make the most of them and don't miss out on opportunities that are presented to you. *See also* Drink.

Teapot

A dream of a teapot suggests that you are likely to form new friendships. If you meet someone you like, take the initiative to make sure you keep in touch. Otherwise you may lose an opportunity.

Tear

See Crying.

Telephone

To dream of receiving or making a telephone call signifies potential; you may become involved in something lucrative.

Telescope

Preoccupation with what does not concern you and things you have no power to change is indicated by dreaming of looking through a telescope. You would do better to concentrate on events and circumstances you can influence. Otherwise you could find that these also move outside your sphere of influence.

Theatre

To dream that you are in a theatre is often an indication of some degree of unreality affecting your life, or perhaps that you have done something you would like to go back to and change, but cannot do so.

Thief

To dream of thieves denotes loss and trouble.

Thigh

The thighs represent the relations, so if you dream that you have broken or injured your legs at the thigh, then a member of your family is likely to experience a problem, not necessarily physical, or you yourself could be annoyed or troubled by a relation. Strong thighs suggest a promotion for a member of the family, or that they might help you to a promotion. *See also* Leg.

Thimble

Dreaming of a thimble suggests an improvement at work.

Thin

Appearing to be very thin in a dream generally suggests that you are likely to have problems, perhaps associated with money.

Thirst

If you dream that you are thirsty and cannot quench your thirst, it suggests that you have a need for something that is not being fulfilled. It could relate to emotional issues, money or a work-related project. If you quench your thirst in a dream with clear, fresh water, you are likely to resolve the issues, although if the water is dirty or polluted, your course in life may not run so smoothly. *See also* Drink.

Thorn

Thorns are symbolic of problems. To find a thorn in your foot suggests that actions you are taking could lead to problems, or that you may not be happy when decisions you have taken come to fruition. If it is too late to change things, there are usually other ways to make the most of the way things have turned out.

Throat

Seeing yourself having your throat cut, or cutting someone else's throat, in a dream indicates an injury, not necessarily physical. If the wound is not fatal, then you, or the injured person, should find the means to overcome the problem.

Throne

A throne is a symbol of responsibility, so if you are sitting on a throne, then you are likely to feel confident that you are able to take responsibility in your life. If the throne is empty, you may have reservations, while if someone else is on the throne, they could represent an authority figure in your life.

Thumb

To dream that you have injured your thumb indicates that you will shortly be in a serious quandary. You may have to choose between giving offence to someone whom it would pay you to please, and making yourself look ridiculous in the eyes of your acquaintances.

Thunder

The sound of thunder without a storm or rain can be a sign of envy, jealousy or unkind rumours. It can also indicate unexpected news. Thunder and lightning together tend to suggest better news or an improvement in your circumstances. *See also* Lightning, Rain, Storm.

Tiger

A tiger is a symbol of power that can be positive but can also be destructive. Being caught by a tiger suggests problems and danger, although if you manage to escape it implies that you should eventually be successful. *See also* Animal.

Tiredness

If you feel tired in a dream, it can be interpreted to mean that you may have to work hard to achieve your ambitions but that you have the necessary attributes to get what you want in life. It may not be an easy path, but it should be worth the effort. *See also* Asleep, Yawn.

Toad

To dream of fighting with toads indicates success. *See also* Frog.

Tomb

Tombs indicate the end of one thing, which can always be seen as the beginning of another if you look forward rather than back.

Tool

A dream featuring tools is related to craft skills or working with your hands in some way. Have you, or has someone close to you, been trying to make a decision about a career path? Do you need to call in the skills of a professional to solve a problem? *See also* individual tools.

Tooth

Teeth are symbolic of your closest relations and friends, so if they appear white and healthy, then you can expect good news and strong friendships, or perhaps that you will benefit from your association. If they are damaged or some are missing, then the implication is that some difficulties will be experienced in relation to someone close to you. If any of your teeth appears so large that it prevents you from eating or speaking, this suggests an argument involving your family.

Torch

Shining a torch is a good sign, one suggesting improvement or a new understanding of your circumstances. If your torch goes out and you cannot switch it on again, you may have some problems resolving your next step. Try to focus objectively on the problem in hand and the solution may not be as difficult to find. Take one step at a time. *See also* Lamp, Light.

Tortoise

A tortoise is a traditional image of long life and success through perseverance. *See also* Animal.

Train

If you dream that you see a train travelling quickly, it suggests a long journey could be unpleasant. *See also* Railway ticket.

Trap

If you have a dream about any kind of trap – whether literally an animal trap, or a plan to trap someone – it is generally an unsettling dream suggesting something unexpected.

Treasure

To dream you discover treasure is a dream image suggesting that you will place your confidence in someone who might let you down. If you dream that you are searching for treasure, you may be concerned that you need to make some major changes in your life, perhaps involving travel. *See also* Digging, Fortune, Gold.

Tree

A healthy tree is a very potent dream image of strength and growth, and is usually a sign of enjoyment, pleasure and comfort. If the tree is in blossom, it suggests success and happiness, either in your relationships, at work, or in your travels. If the trees are dried up, diseased, uprooted or damaged, however, then it is possible that your own enjoyment may suffer a similar downturn, perhaps through outside influences or perhaps through your own mismanagement of the situation, depending on the circumstances in the dream. Planting trees is a promising dream image, as it can indicate that you are laying the foundations for future success, even though you may have to wait some time to reap the benefits. Watching trees growing also indicates a potentially good future, and that you are moving in the right direction to achieve what you want in life. Cutting down trees is often seen as a sign of potential loss. *See also* individual trees.

Trout

The dream image of a trout suggests that you will be able to overcome the next obstacle that is placed in your path. *See also* Fish.

Trumpet

Trumpets sounding are symbolic of arguments and aggressive behaviour. You should be able to control your own temper and behave more considerately towards others. If you become aware that other people are behaving in an increasingly aggressive way, try to calm the situation down and prevent it getting out of control. *See also* Music.

Tumbler

To dream that you drink from a clean tumbler denotes health and activity; from a dirty one, the reverse.

Tunnel

To dream that you are in a tunnel and feel afraid is a sign that you could soon make a wrong decision in a matter of some importance unless you are careful to take stock and weigh up all the arguments. If you can see light at the end of the tunnel, you can be reassured that you will eventually make the right decision.

Turtledove

To dream of turtledoves suggests that you are confident in the affection you receive from those close to you. *See also* Bird.

Twins

Dreaming of twins is said to suggest that every question can have two sides that can be made to work in harmony with the right attitude.

Ulcer

Dreaming of mouth ulcers relates to eloquence and the ability of the person suffering from the ulcers in the dream to be able to communicate well in some way, through speech, music or acting.

Umbrella

An umbrella is a protective symbol in a dream. If you are sheltering under an umbrella, you should be protected from difficulties. If you tear or break your umbrella, you may be heading for some problems; perhaps you will be blamed for something you didn't do, or find that you are lacking in support when you most need it. If you are given an umbrella, look out for good advice from a friend or colleague. To dream that you lose your umbrella is a sign that you are likely to receive a gift.

Underground

If you are underground in a dream, you may be feeling the need to explore your own unconscious, the real needs and desires that are driving you, rather than focusing on the more superficial issues in life.

Unemployment

This could suggest that you are feeling undervalued or inadequate and unable to face the tasks ahead of you. Try to assess your positive talents rather than focusing on the negative.

Unfaithfulness

To dream that someone, especially your partner, is unfaithful to you suggests that you are confident they will remain trustworthy, even though you may be aware of temptations they are facing.

Unicorn

A symbol of purity and innocence, while you need to be aware of its importance in your life, it is important not to forget that the real world needs attention as well.

University

Any kind of university or further education institution in a dream is a suggestion that you should think about how you can advance your education in order to get ahead in your life. It does not necessarily mean you should go to college. It might suggest you broaden your life skills, read more, become better informed, or expand your horizons in any way.

Vegetable

To dream of vegetables is an indication of unrewarded work; to gather vegetables signifies quarrels, and to eat them indicates loss in business. *See also* individual vegetables.

Veil

Seeing someone wearing a veil, or wearing one yourself, has implications of hidden motives and dishonesty.

Velvet

Velvet is a rich fabric that promises pleasure and wealth. If it is black, the advantage is more likely to be in the professional sphere; if it is red, look to personal gain. *See also* Clothes.

Venison

To dream about venison denotes change in affairs. To dream you eat it suggests you may encounter problems. *See also* Deer, Eating.

Vermin

To dream of vermin indicates an unwarranted influence in your affairs, perhaps by someone who wants to break up a relationship. *See also* individual vermin.

Vine

Vines symbolise abundance and fertility. Things are likely to run very smoothly for some time to come.

Vinegar

Dreaming of drinking vinegar suggests illness, deceit or problems with a relationship.

Violet

Violets are positive omens and suggest your love and respect are returned. If they are out of season, they indicate a newly awakened affection. *See also* Flower.

Violin

To dream you play or see someone else play a violin signifies good news, harmony and good relationships with others. *See also* Music.

Virgin Mary

To dream that you speak to the Holy Virgin Mary signifies consolation, recovery of health and good fortune. To dream you talk with her signifies joy.

Visit

To dream of receiving a visit implies that you might benefit from being friendly with new acquaintances as you are likely to meet someone who could be a considerable help to you.

Voice

To dream you hear a voice but cannot see who is speaking is a suggestion that you could be deluded by a con artist. Perhaps you tend to be too naïve or trusting for your own good.

Volcano

If you dream about a volcanic eruption, it suggests serious change.

Vulture

A vulture signifies a dangerous enemy, especially if it is eating its prey. If you kill one, it suggests you will have the presence of mind to overcome any difficulties you encounter. *See also* Bird of prey.

Walking

To dream of walking in the dirt or among thorns is a dream image suggesting illness. To dream you walk in rushing water signifies adversity, or at night signifies trouble and melancholy. To dream you walk in a forest signifies trouble. To walk in a garden or on holy ground signifies joy. To dream that you are walking in a crowd which drops away until you are alone suggests that you might give offence to people, but you have to act in accordance with your conscience.

Walnut

Seeing walnuts in a dream can be an indication of difficulty or hard work ahead, although if you crack and eat them successfully and they taste good, this is a good indication of success. *See also* Nut.

War

To dream of war signifies trouble and anger, although if you fight and win it suggests difficulties can be avoided or overcome.

Washing

If you have a dream in which you are washing, it suggests that you are moving on to a new phase and doing away with what has gone before. If the water is fresh and clean, there is an especially positive move ahead. This also applies if you are bathing in the clear water of a river or a lake. *See also* Bath.

Wasp

To dream you are stung by a wasp signifies anxiety and trouble caused by envious people. *See also* Sting.

Watch

To dream that your watch has stopped suggests an end to something, perhaps a relationship.

Water

Water is generally thought to suggest the course of your life, so if you dream that you see a clear, calm stretch of water, this indicates good times ahead, while if it is rough, muddy or polluted, things may not look so good. *See also* Fountain, Lake, Pond, River, Sea, Swimming, Well.

Watermill

This is a favourable dream omen indicating profitable change.

Wave

Waves on the sea or on a lake are indicative of life in general and having to cope with both the good and the bad. To dream of crashing waves on a shore is considered to be a sign that you must be prepared to fight for what you want.

Weasel

The fact that the word 'weasel' has a pejorative connotation indicates how the image is traditionally viewed. In a dream, it is considered a sign that you should be wary of other people's motives. *See also* Animal.

Wedding

Dreaming of a wedding is most common if you are actually involved in wedding arrangements in real life, in which case it indicates only a preoccupation with the event and some nervousness about it. For people with no other connections with weddings, it is traditionally considered a negative image in a dream, and one that suggests that you need to think about making some changes in your life to improve your prospects. *See also* Elopement, Marriage, Wedding ring.

Wedding ring

A wedding ring is a potent symbol of relationships, and the circumstances of the dream may indicate the particular significance. If it is lost and then found, for example, it can indicate that you may have problems in your relationship but that they can be overcome.

Weed

A mass of weeds in a dream is indicative of blighted hopes, although if you are working to clear the weeds, then you are someone who tends to work hard to overcome difficulties and is usually successful. *See also* Gardening.

Weighing

To dream of weighing anything on a scales suggests that you will soon accept that you must take advantage of the benefits you have, rather than wishing that you possessed something else.

Well

Dreaming of drawing water from a well suggests that you or your partner is likely to become well known for your wisdom or expertise. If the water is muddy, there may be troubles ahead. *See also* Water.

Whale

Being able to cope with an environment that is foreign to most mammals, the whale becomes a symbol of coping with unusual circumstances and mastering them.

Wheat

To dream you see a field of wheat is an image of money and profit gained through hard work.

Whispering

To hear whispering in a dream suggests that many people are talking about you behind your back, and that you should be sure that they do not have good reason to do so.

Widow/widower

To dream that you are a widow or widower is a sign of disappointments in love or problematic relationships.

Will

To dream that you make your will is a sign of a long and happy life. *See also* Bequest, Executor.

Wind

To dream that you are being buffeted by a strong wind is thought to be an indication that you will soon have a battle on your hands. You will need firmness and determination to get through. *See also* Hurricane.

Wind instrument

To dream of playing or hearing a wind instrument played is traditionally thought to indicate that you will have to face difficulties. *See also* Music.

Window

Looking out of a window at a landscape is often seen as a sign that you are likely to undertake a journey, or perhaps step out on a new direction in life. Shuttered, broken or damaged windows can indicate limited options or that you have to find new opportunities.

Wine

Dreaming of drinking wine socially tends to be an indication of good health, or of improved finances, although if you overindulge it suggests that you should think about taking greater care. Perhaps you are not paying enough attention to health, or perhaps you or your relatives are being careless with money. *See also* Champagne, Drink.

Wing

A broken wing suggests that you feel something is holding you back, while having wings indicates a feeling of freedom and an ability to move on. *See also* Flying.

Winner

Dreaming that you are the winner in any kind of competition suggests that however hard you study and practise, you are more suited to physical rather than intellectual pursuits.

Witch

The traditional interpretation of dreaming about a witch is that strangers will be present in your life. Perhaps you will go on a journey, strangers may enter your life, or you may be dependent on a stranger for support.

Wolf

The wolf is a symbol of an avaricious, cruel and disloyal person. If you are bitten by a wolf in a dream, you may be robbed or injured – not necessarily physically – by such a person, but if you overcome the wolf, you are likely to gain the upper hand in real life. *See also* Animal.

Wood

A dream in which you are carrying wood signifies profit, while if you are chopping wood it suggests a happy family. Carrying wood on your back symbolises success through hard work and heavy responsibilities. *See also* Forest, Sawing.

Wool

Wool is a dream image suggesting that you will have all the material things you need. *See also* Clothes.

Working

If you dream that you are hard at work, you should think carefully about your employment situation and ensure that you are, in reality, doing everything you can to do a good job.

Workman

If you see someone in your dream who is working hard, especially in a workshop or factory, it suggests a promise that your own hard work will be financially profitable.

Worm

An image of worms in a dream suggests that someone close to you is trying to undermine you. It may relate to problems in the family, or someone acting against your best interests while trying to appear to be a friend or colleague.

Wound

Stab wounds, especially on the body, suggest that the attacker will act in an extraordinarily beneficial way towards the person attacked.

Wren

To dream of these tiny British hedgerow birds is a symbol of contentment, especially in your romantic relationships. *See also* Bird.

Writing

Dreaming of writing is suggestive of communication. Perhaps you may receive news; perhaps you have been thinking about someone who wants to hear from you. To see handwriting in a dream suggests that you will soon learn something that may not necessarily be pleasant. If you are writing with the hand you do not usually write with, it indicates that there is a degree of deception involved, either on your part or on that of the person you are thinking about. *See also* Letter.

X-ray

This image in a dream suggests that something is likely to happen that will give you more of an insight into an important decision.

Xylophone

Accidents in the home are possible if you dream of a xylophone. *See also* Music.

Yacht

If you dream of sailing a yacht, or watching a yacht sailing, it is believed to suggest change in your life, perhaps involving some considerable element of risk. *See also* Boat.

Yawn

If you are continuously yawning in your dream, it is a clear sign that you are lacking energy in your life. Perhaps you are bored with your current job and should begin to look further afield; perhaps you need to look to your general health and well-being and find ways of improving them. *See also* Tiredness.

Yew tree

Because of its traditional associations, a yew tree as a prominent feature in a dream is generally considered contrary to the normal interpretation of a tree in a dream, suggesting loss. *See also* Tree.

Yorkshire pudding

This is a homely image in a dream indicating domestic happiness and contentment. *See also* Eating.

Zebra

A zebra is not considered a particularly promising dream image. It is thought to be a sign that you may disagree with those around you, or that you may be disappointed when you finally reach the goal you have been striving towards.

Zip

This represents openness or closure in dealings with other people.

Zoo

Visiting a zoo in a dream is a good image, as it suggests successful relationships and a positive outlook on life. *See also* Animal.

Index

abroad 15, 37, 72, 90, 119
  news from 88, 140, 154, 169
  see also journey; travel
accidents 7, 11, 45, 60, 143, 165
  at home 73, 166, 187
alcohol 36–7, 41, 89, 92, 144, 185
attack 15, 23, 43, 53, 151, 186
authority 42, 51, 62, 116
  figure of 61, 146, 172

bites 23, 84, 149, 162, 185
buildings 30, 35, 41, 136, 144, 153
  houses 62, 79, 100–1, 124, 151

calm 15, 32, 70, 122, 132, 152, 168
  water 25, 152, 154, 156, 165
children 8, 44, 92, 133, 134
  having 55, 78, 112, 132, 152
  playing 39, 88, 92, 129
  problems with 77, 96
  young 4, 16, 40, 92
colours 23–4, 43, 82, 107, 144, 178
communication 37, 88, 95, 103
  verbal 40, 47, 137, 146, 163, 176
  written 69, 127, 139, 187
  see also reading; writing
control 7, 81, 137
  lack of 14, 100, 101, 144, 146
  manipulated 27, 118, 144, 149

danger 103, 107, 110, 115, 172, 180
death 48, 55, 87, 98, 108
  burial 30, 45, 93, 173
drink 63, 67, 171, 179, 183
  alcohol 37, 41, 89, 144, 185
  hot 44, 45, 162, 169
  jugs for 32, 90, 106, 175

eating 38, 130, 136, 152, 162, 181
  and animals 62, 67, 154, 178, 180
  fruit 12, 13, 92, 132
  hunger 66, 75, 101, 173
  meals 28, 59, 76, 120, 188
  sweets 40, 144, 168
  valuables 58, 160
  vegetables 36, 88, 98, 138, 178
education 17, 41, 118, 155, 177
  see also reading; skills
employment 22, 68, 69, 78, 177
  jobs 43, 68–9, 76, 151
enemies 11, 61, 65
  powerful 21, 25, 117, 180
envy 41, 47, 69, 78–9, 84, 95
  image of 97, 105, 115, 161, 172
  see also jealousy
extravagance 110, 133, 149, 159, 163

falling 74, 83, 99, 156, 164
  to ground 60, 124, 143, 145, 151

Index

fame 15, 63, 64, 74
family 14, 104, 116, 152
  happy 76, 108, 133
  problems 29, 135, 165, 170, 173
fear 76, 83, 88–9, 116, 157, 175
fertility 100, 140, 149, 165, 166
  trees and 112, 133, 179
fire 123, 151, 161
flattery 50, 59, 80, 103, 132
  image of 84, 87
flying 20, 108, 123
birds 64, 83, 111, 140
  fraud 29, 71, 86, 164, 180
freedom 54, 62, 132, 136, 185
friends 22, 33, 45, 86, 117
  absent 6, 65, 75, 166
  false 9, 12, 50, 107, 120
  influential 10, 116
  new 65, 75, 90, 137
  old 30, 41, 60, 91, 92
  respect of 26, 59
  true 37, 70, 86, 94, 105, 108
  trust in 15, 60, 80

gifts 40, 89, 165, 176
  of value 105, 122–3, 126, 150
gossip 65, 80, 87, 93, 119, 137

home 15, 18, 39, 87, 107, 161
humour 92, 126, 128, 136, 148

influence 10, 19, 95, 147, 178
  on life 37, 47, 113, 116
inheritance 21, 34, 100, 126
injury 31, 33, 103, 155, 160, 186
  animal 149, 151, 162, 164, 185

arm 14, 78, 79, 96, 172
body 45, 104, 149
head 22, 65, 116, 128, 171, 177
leg 84, 109, 113, 170, 171

jealousy 23, 74, 100, 105, 115, 172
  and colour 43, 68, 132
jewellery 29, 65, 126, 150, 182
jewels 9, 58, 68, 78, 105, 132
journey 19, 106, 110, 184, 185
  pleasant 98, 119, 147, 164, 167
  unwanted 69, 135, 174

laziness 13, 14, 64, 141
life 67, 74, 106, 174
  long 30, 73, 108, 128, 174, 184
  new 16, 19, 40–1, 66, 167
love 23, 35, 46, 75, 166, 179
  romantic 18, 117, 150, 159, 187
  stable 19, 67, 79, 115
  unhappy 27, 38, 85, 112, 183
  see also marriage; partners; sex
lovers 49, 139

madness 11, 15, 103, 118
marriage 43, 55, 68, 69, 120
  happy 19, 100, 165, 167
  weddings 100, 131, 182
money 22, 45, 91, 122–3
  caution 19, 58, 110, 133, 185
  images 7, 59, 183
  loss 16, 55, 58, 85, 93, 123
  much 17, 21, 76, 126
  problems 151, 171
  savings 10, 74, 78
music 46, 125, 133, 176

Index

instruments 63, 187
  string 94, 97, 140, 179
  wind 17, 82, 175, 184
  singing 40, 64, 132, 160

opportunities 65, 139, 155
  missed 67, 81, 161, 169
  new 52, 62, 87, 101, 147
  wasted 28, 64, 143

parents 8, 126, 135, 137, 151
  fathers 75, 108
  mothers 4, 28, 108, 123
partners 59, 68, 90, 92, 115, 133
  difficult 54, 80, 99, 132, 151
  finding 23, 64, 70, 87, 90, 128
  happy 67, 134, 138, 150, 177
power 42, 103, 145
  animal 62, 67, 97, 116–17, 172
  head image for 100, 126, 128
  and sex 35, 151, 162
promotion 35, 39, 59, 69, 170

reading 69, 148, 177
  print 8, 26, 118, 127–8, 130
religion 3, 72, 90, 122, 143
  Bible 26, 137, 161
  Christianity 40–1, 46, 50, 179
  churches 10, 35, 41, 47
  prayer 41, 90, 143
  spirit of 3, 20, 54, 72, 83, 145
rivals 29, 64, 68, 69, 86, 103, 150
rumour 27, 65, 80, 84, 172

secrets 68, 101, 137, 141–2, 158
  hidden 52, 88, 132
sex 8, 81, 100, 130, 144
  homosexuality 99, 157
  power and 35, 151, 162
skills 65, 142, 147, 163, 177
  new 113, 115, 118
  practical 56, 121, 173
slander 21, 65, 80, 84
strangers 57, 68, 73, 129, 166, 185
  gain from 56, 133
  trust of 22, 50, 53

talents 26, 40, 56, 114, 121, 177
  artistic 29, 34
  creative 66, 82, 88, 107, 157
travel 19, 25, 91, 100, 104, 119
  afar 72, 99, 154, 174
  images 36, 62, 94, 110, 157

walking 93, 138
  in grass 44, 77, 88, 180
  hampered 27, 51, 146, 180
  near water 29, 32, 157
  in trees 85, 106, 133
warning 29, 82, 115, 118, 156
  behaviour 40, 61, 143
  money 22, 76, 85, 93
washing 20, 35, 73, 84, 181
water 20, 25, 32–3, 181
  activity 60, 63, 81, 168, 180
  features 32–3, 86, 110, 142, 183
  river 25, 33, 150, 152
  sea 154, 156, 158–9, 182, 188
  see also drink; washing
weather 81, 94, 147, 162, 165, 166
  storm 101, 115, 147, 156, 165
women 4, 27, 28, 40, 66, 108, 123
writing 8, 69, 114, 127, 141, 187